TIGERS

A Look Into The Glittering Eye

LEE SERVER

PORTLAND HOUSE

NEW YORK

This 1991 edition published by Portland House, distributed by Outlet Book Company, Inc., a Random House Company, 225 Park Avenue South, New York, New York 10003.

This book was designed and produced by Todtri Productions Limited P.O. Box 20058 New York, NY 10023-1482

Printed and Bound in Singapore

Library of Congress Catalog Card Number 90-63351

ISBN 0-517-05691-7
8 7 6 5 4 3 2 1

Author: Lee Server
Producer: Robert M. Tod
Designer and Art Director: Mark Weinberg
Editor: Mary Forsell
Typeset and Page Makeup: Strong Silent Type/NYC

TABLE OF CONTENTS

INTRODUCTION

The tiger is one of nature's masterpieces. A creature of beauty and grace, it rivals only man in its power and cunning. Whether encountered only through the bars of a zoo's enclosure, or glimpsed in the wild as it stalks its night's prey with silent footfalls, eyes red like fire, the sight of this great cat is not easily forgotten. The tiger's body is thickly yet exquisitely designed, the steely muscles in back and shoulders rippling in movement, the huge legs propelling it so smoothly and quietly that it seems at times to be gliding above the jungle floor. It is the largest of all the felines, some measuring up to thirteen feet long and weighing as much as seven hundred pounds. Its powerful canine teeth nearly the size of a man's finger can kill even large prey in an instant, and it has been known to bring down adversaries as big as the elephant and the rhinoceros. When the tiger is on the prowl, the atmosphere in the forest is charged and the air crackles with assorted cries of danger.

Until this century, the tiger was uncontested ruler of its domain, an invincible predatory monarch. It reigned supreme not just in its legendary habitat, the wilds of India, but in the jungles and mangroves of southeast Asia, the snowbound conifer forests of Siberia, and the steppes and mountains beyond the Caspian Sea—across nearly every corner of the Asian continent from Turkey in the west to Korea in the east.

Those times for the tiger are no more. There were once eight subspecies, or races, of tigers in the world. No comprehensive data exists, but it is estimated that the tiger population before 1900 numbered in the hundreds of thousands. Now several subspecies--the Caspian tiger, the Javan tiger, the Balinese tiger—are extinct, gone forever. Of the five remaining subspecies (the Bengal, Chinese, Corbett's, Siberian, and Sumatran), the Chinese tiger is down to perilously low numbers, and in the wild, the Siberian remains at great risk, with perhaps only two hundred tigers remaining. The total population of non-captive tigers in their natural habitat is now approximately nine thousand. And yet these are hopeful numbers compared to statistics of a few decades ago, when the Bengals of India were less than half their current number, and there were no more than thirty Siberian tigers left in the wild.

How did an animal of such superior strength and resourcefulness come to the brink of annihilation in the course of a few decades? From the time of their first meeting, mankind has feared and felt in awe of the great Asian predator. When the English poet William Blake wrote, "What immortal hand or eye/Has framed thy fearful symmetry?" he represented those who rhapsodized over the cat's savage beauty and majesty. But far more often the tiger stood for all the "treachery" and "wanton cruelty" of the untamed wilderness. Indeed, while humans are not the natural prey of this animal, many thousands of men and women have been killed by tigers, a situation that continues to the present day. And yet the man-eating tiger is a virtual aberration compared to man's lethal aggressiveness toward the tiger. We have killed them directly—slaughtering the cats for sport or to make expensive coats from their pelts—and indirectly—squeezing them from their habitat through ecological destruction and the encroachments of civilization.

As human populations have grown and expanded and business and government interests have moved in search of new resources to exploit, the tiger's wilderness domain has been disrupted and often destroyed. For many years the killing of wildlife and the clearing of jungle and forest were considered marks of progress in primitive areas. The mere thinning of forests for timber in parts of India has been a sufficient enough factor to interfere with the delicate balance of the wilderness ecosystem, in which each element of that system is dependent upon the rest.

While the tiger has proven adaptable to certain changes in its environment, the upheavals of the past fifty years have been massive. In India, for example, the amount of forested land has dropped from over seventy-five percent of the total to less than twenty percent. The tiger is a solitary creature, and each individual cat is meant to function in the wild within its own marked territory. Once the habitat has shrunk beyond the point where it can support the tiger's individual range, the tigers in that area will begin to die out.

Signs of the tiger's threatened existence were known for some time, but ignored. Legendary hunter-turned-conservationist Jim Corbett, an Englishman born and raised in India, noted that for every one hundred tigers he had seen at the turn of the century, there was one by the 1930s. Corbett attempted to make the colonial authorities aware of the importance of the Indian wildlife. But little was done by the British or by the subsequent government after India's independence. It was not until the 1970s, when reports of the Indian tiger's struggle for survival caused worldwide alarm, that drastic action was taken.

The World Wildlife Fund and the International Union for the Conservation of Nature and Natural Resources joined forces with the Indian government in a rescue effort called Project Tiger. The project's task force proposed to eliminate many of the factors contributing to the tiger's dire straits, such as destruction of habitat, hunting, and poaching. The tiger's plight was of utmost importance, but the project was also concerned with total environmental preservation. Nine locations were chosen as tiger reserves. In the beginning, the project faced serious opposition from many Indian states, which preferred to harvest timber and otherwise exploit their wilderness areas. There were other unpopular aspects to the project. Numerous villages would have to be relocated outside the new sanctuaries. For many rural Indians, themselves in a day-to-day struggle for survival, the care and attention being paid to what were regarded as man-eating beasts seemed an outrage.

Royal Tiger (*Felis tigris*). From photo. by Dixon, London.

It would take some time and effort to convince these villagers that the wilderness reserves were important, if not merely in the cause of ecology and an endangered species, then for the much-needed foreign capital they would produce from international tourism. It was hoped that the tourists would also more directly benefit the populace financially in the vicinity of the game reserves.

In certain parts of India the tiger has not helped his own cause any by attacking and killing both tourists and locals. An average of fifty people are killed by tigers every year. But most of these incidents are tragic errors, humans unwittingly surprising a tiger in the undergrowth or a tigress protecting her cubs. The incidents of marauding man-eaters hunting for human flesh, or even of tigers attacking human beings who are clearly identified, walking upright on an open path or road, are more legend than fact. But make no mistake, the tiger can be an extremely brutal and dangerous animal, capable of ferociously defending what it perceives as its territory. If a tiger has been displaced, or its territory altered so that traditional prey species have disappeared and been replaced by the presence of humans, a tiger will attack man to survive. In the past, tiger attacks have been much more numerous. One cat alone, the legendary Champawat tigress, killed over four hundred people before she was shot. Tiger attacks were another factor leading to the animal's decline, since people would hunt and slaughter great numbers of them in the name of safety or revenge. Part of the goal of the conservationists is to establish protected areas where nature is undisturbed and the tiger will contentedly stalk only its natural prey.

In India, the government has had to come up with new methods of dealing with problem tigers and with consoling frightened or angry villagers when a violent incident has occurred—methods other than sending hunters out to kill any or all likely marauders. When a tiger breaches the border of a reserve and kills a buffalo or bullock, the government compensates the farmer for the loss. When a tiger takes a human victim, a larger compensation is paid. These payments range from two hundred to five hundred dollars, and are, quite understandably, not always considered sufficient for the loss of a farmer's only livestock or the death of a family member. (Incidentally, if a farm animal is killed within the sanctuary grounds, its owner is not compensated, and anyone caught killing a tiger is fined—for an amount that usually exceeds the human-death compensation—and sent to jail.)

One area of India where tigers have for some time been inordinately aggressive toward man is the southeastern region of mangrove swamp and forested islands known as the Sundarbans. This area, part of which reaches into Bangladesh, is the largest single reserve of tigers in the world—and the most dangerous. For hundreds of years, fishermen and foragers who have entered the Sundarbans to fish, hunt, or gather wood have been savagely attacked. Repeatedly, tigers have actually charged into the boats to reach their human prey. In recent years, an average of fifty people have been killed annually just in the Sundarbans region alone. The government was called on to end its conservation plans and restrictions there and to allow the tigers to be eliminated or further restricted. Conservationists and officials investigated the situation. Why did this one region show such a high incidence of aggressive attacks on man?

The answers they came up with were further proof that the tiger's behavior patterns were not unpredictable or "irrational," but part of a complex natural interaction with its environment. Tigers spray scent markings on the boundaries of their territory, alerting other tigers and other predators not to trespass. It was found that many of these markings were washed away by the strong tides in the Sundarbans, which may have left the tigers feeling unsure of each other's territory and therefore guarded and belligerent. Other evidence showed that the tigers' aggressiveness may have had its root in the highly saline water of the area, the salt water irritating the cats' livers. And even with these special circumstances at work, the researchers found that only a small percentage of the Sundarbans tiger population took part in the aggressive attacks on people.

Conservation officials introduced a series of nonlethal solutions to the murderous situation in the Sundarbans. To offset the possible disruptive effects of the salt water, the government dug a number of freshwater pools. Because tigers tend not to attack their prey from the front, the government issued the local fishermen clay and plastic face masks. The masks, worn on the back of the head, are meant to confuse the tigers as they stalk the fishermen from behind. Finally, the government installed electrified clay dummies in the forest. The dummies, decked out in some of the local villagers' old clothes, were wired to give off a two-hundred-volt electric shock when touched. The theory was that once a tiger had received a blistering shock from attacking one of the humanlike dummies, it would tend to avoid humans in the future. It is not possible to determine precisely how well the electric "therapy" worked, but many of the clay dummies had been attacked. At any rate, this combination of projects added up to a fifty-percent drop in the number of men killed by tigers in the Sundarbans. It was believed that programs educating the surrounding residents would bring this figure down even more. This case was important in the progress of tiger conservation, proving that solutions could be found for even a dangerous and aggressive situation that did not have to involve the barrel of a rifle. The Sundarbans continues to be one of the best hopes for the future of the Bengal tiger.

Overall, Project Tiger has been a great success. The number of tigers in India has doubled in the twenty years since the project began. The nine original game reserves continue to thrive, while six more parks have been created. There is now more than twenty-five thousand square kilometers of government-protected land for India's endangered wildlife. In neighboring Nepal, another home to the Bengal tiger, the conservation-minded monarchy has brought fifteen percent of the country's total forest area under government protection. Through the project, the plight of the tiger captured the interest of people everywhere, and donations arrived from around the world, helping to fund the project's costly goals. In many of the sanctuaries, the work done to save the tiger helped save and rehabilitate the habitat itself. In the process of saving the great predator, many other animals received protection and reversed their own move toward the endangered list. The Asian elephant and the rhinoceros are among the species immeasurably helped by the progress of Project Tiger. Despite great pressures directed against its involvement, the Indian government has provided more than half the funds for the tiger reserves and is developing a tourist industry that will generate the future funds to maintain these vast wilderness areas, a brave position in a poor and overcrowded nation.

But it is too soon to declare victory for the tiger. The long-term prognosis is still not good. Even the largest of the Indian reserves are still mere enclaves, islands of natural habitat surrounded by an ever-developing world, inhibiting significant expansion. For the tiger subspecies found in other parts of Asia—notably Siberia, China, and Sumatra—this situation is even more critical.

The tiger is a solitary and mysterious creature. In the following pages, I will try to unravel a bit of the tiger's mystery, to detail its nature and history, and to discuss the work being done to try and ensure that this magnificent animal does not disappear. Could anyone disagree that a world without tigers would be a poor place indeed?

PORTRAIT OF A PREDATOR

While the tiger is most often thought of as a denizen of the tropical jungle, its actual origins are in the cold, snowbound areas of northern Asia, perhaps as far north as the lower Arctic. At some time in the ancient past, the tiger migrated south, throughout the Orient and the Indian subcontinent, and east to Turkey and Iran. It has lived in habitats of great ecological diversity and has evolved into a number of distinct subspecies, with individual modifications. Tigers from the original, northern habitat—the Siberian subspecies—are the largest tigers and have a considerably thicker coat to conserve body heat in the frigid winters of their homeland. Farther south the tiger becomes smaller, its coat thinner. The Siberian tiger measures up to thirteen feet in length, while the Bengal tiger of India has an average length of ten feet. The "island tigers" of Sumatra and Bali, still farther south, have an average length of eight feet.

Although tropic-habitat tigers have a much lighter coat than their Siberian cousins, the animals' northern origins are still felt in hot climates. The Bengal tiger will try to spend blazing hot days lying in shade or in some cooling water. If forced to move around in the midday sun, the tiger will pant heavily, its lolling tongue hanging out. Curiously, the Siberian tiger's typical tawny and black striped coat is more appropriate for the jungle topography of the south, where it can blend in with the grass and undergrowth for camouflage, than for the white winter landscapes of the far north.

It is the Indian, or Bengal, tiger that makes the most flexible use of its coat and markings. The Indian subcontinent has a wide variety of landscapes and temperatures, from the snowy forests of the Himalayas to the swampy Sundarbans to the parched scrubs of Rajasthan, and the Bengal tiger has adapted to each environment. The tiger's color and markings are amazingly able to fulfill the same camouflage function in a variety of geographical conditions. To see this distinctive animal unobstructed, with its bold color and unique pattern of stripes, it is hard to believe how it can blend in so efficiently in such a range of surroundings. In tall grass the tiger's body blends in with the stalks and its stripes become their shadows. In a forest of bamboo, the tiger seems indistinguishable from the yellow bamboo. In the brown and yellow world of the deciduous forest, the tiger is again virtually invisible. This effect occurs even when you are within a few yards of the animal. In the game parks, visitors are often dependent on an experienced guide to point out the giant cats even when they are looking directly at the animal. Even when you have discerned the tiger's outline in the foliage, it can shift slightly and disappear again.

While it might seem to the casual observer that all tigers have similar—even identical—coloration and markings, there is a wide if relatively subtle range of colors, and in fact no two tigers have exactly the same markings. The markings are not even symmetrical—despite poet William Blake's tribute—on an individual tiger from its left side to its right. Stripes may be thinner or become spots. The number of variations is infinite.

Similarly, there is no uniform color to the tiger's coat. The fur ranges from a very light orange to dark shades of red and ocher. Certain areas—throat, chest, muzzle, stomach, and the insides of the legs—are colored various shades of white. The stripes may be reduced on the forelegs and shoulders. White tigers are rare—the first specimen was caught only in 1820—and white Siberians rarer still, but white Bengals have been found in many areas of India. Some are a dazzling pure white, with eyes of pale pink. More often they are an off-white with brown or black stripes and cold-blue eyes.

At first it was believed that they were a separate race of tiger, but they are actually albinos with a mutant gene. The white tigers are born in a litter with tigers of normal coloration. Still, they have long been an object of fascination and even superstition. In the kingdom of Assam, there is a long-held belief that a person who sees a white tiger will soon die.

The White Tigers of Rewa

A white tiger dynasty of sorts began in the central Indian state of Rewa. More white tigers had turned up in this area, now part of Madhya Pradesh, than anywhere else on record. In 1915, the local maharajah caught a white cub and kept it until its death, then stuffed it and sent it as a present to Britain's King George V. A later maharajah, Shri Martand Sing, captured another white cub during a shikar, or hunt, that took the life of the cub's mother. The cub was placed in a large, open courtyard of the maharajah's sprawling palace, but it escaped. Only after a long hunt by the shikaris and several violent confrontations was the feisty baby tiger subdued—with a knockout blow to its skull. The male cub was named Mohan and raised with lavish care, as his owner hoped to be the first person ever to breed white tigers.

As an adult, Mohan was mated with a normal Bengal tigress caught for that purpose. The tigress, Begum, bore him several litters, but all had the normal Bengal coloration. The frustrated maharajah then mated Mohan with a daughter from Mohan's second litter. All of Rewa, it seems, held its breath when the time came for the new mate, Radha, to give birth. She bore four cubs: Mohini, Rajs, Rani, and Sukeshi. The genetic mix had produced the desired outcome. All four were white.

One of the females, Sukeshi, was kept at Rewa for mating with Mohan. Raja and Rani were given to the zoo in Delhi and became that zoo's most famous exhibit. Mohini, at the age of two, was purchased by a businessman for ten thousand dollars and given as a present to the children of the United States. The white tigress would live at the National Zoo in Washington, D.C. It took eleven men to carry Mohini from the maharajah's palace to the airstrip, one of them being Dr. Theodore Reed, the National Zoo's director. Reed, well aware of the extreme rarity of the tigress, scarcely let Mohini out of his sight for the entire long journey to America, sleeping only when the tigress did and then stretched out atop her cage. Installed at the zoo, Mohini was beloved by all who saw her. It was not just her rare color but her charm and grace that delighted visitors, and many agreed that if Mohini had been human she would have been a movie star.

The Washington zoo was, of course, interested in breeding more white tigers. Obtaining another white tiger was not possible, but the zoo did find one of Mohini's normal-colored uncles, Samson. One of their offspring then mated with Mohini, and the white gene pool produced a white tigress, Rewati. This cub, though beautiful and healthy, showed signs of "inbreeding depression": her

A CHARGE AGAINST THE NETTING.

blue eyes were crossed, her back was curved, and her legs were short. Tiger-breeding specialists determined it was probably safer to outbreed the white tigers with yellows and mate their offspring with the hope of breeding white cubs.

The Black Tiger Controversy

Is there such a thing as a black tiger? Reports of such tigers have persisted through the years, but evidence has been scant. Reported black cats were shot in at least two areas of India, Chittagong and the Lushai Hills, but the carcasses were never kept for scientific investigation. In China, an American missionary named Harry R. Caldwell, who was well educated in natural history and knowledgeable about the local wildlife, described a clear sighting of a tiger colored deep shades of blue and maltese. He was not able to catch the cat, but locals confirmed to him sightings of numerous "black devils" in the area.

Tigers by Classification

Because the tiger is a secretive and solitary creature, it has been one of the least studied animals, and there has long been a degree of confusion over many aspects of the species. It was once believed that there were many more subspecies of tiger than are now accepted. Through the centuries, scientists have been uncertain how to classify the tiger. It was initially called Felis tigris, then the genus name was changed to Panthera because of the tiger's characteristic roundly contracting pupils and partially ossified hyoid. Other scientists believed Panthera should be applied exclusively to the leopard and jaguar, the spotted cats. Some naturalists lobbied to have the tiger classified as the separate genus of Tigris. There have been eight commonly accepted subspecies of tiger. Three of these are now believed completely extinct.

BALI TIGER (Panthera tigris balica)
Like the Javan and Sumatran, this is another Indonesian "island tiger." Rarely seen, some questioned its existence as a separate subspecies, but it was darker and had fewer stripes than the other Indonesians. The Bali tiger vanished for good in the last five years or so.

BENGAL TIGER (Panthera tigris tigris)
Also known as the Indian tiger, the Bengal tiger was once common on the subcontinent, but became scarce in many regions since the late nineteenth century. It reached the endangered point in the late 1940s, when indiscriminate hunting and habitat destruction were widespread. The Bengal is large, averaging ten feet in length. This tiger was saved from oblivion by a worldwide effort begun in the 1970s. There are now approximately six thousand Bengals living in the wild in India, Nepal, and Bangladesh.

CASPIAN TIGER (Panthera tigris virgata)
Similar in size and color to the Bengal, the Caspian roamed the westernmost range of the tiger, its territory including parts of Afghanistan, Iran, the Soviet Union, and Turkey. This subspecies was known to be dwindling in number since the 1930s. It is now considered extinct, although there are reports of a few tigers still living in a remote part of Afghanistan.

CHINESE TIGER (Panthera tigris amoyensis)
Native to eastern China, the Chinese tiger's habitat has included forest and rocky mountains, and many once lived in caves along the Chinese coast near the island of Amoy. The Chinese tiger has been hunted to the verge of extinction, partly because of a vast market for all sorts of tiger parts used in Oriental rituals and medicines. This tiger is now considered in its biological death throes in the wild. It is found in a few scattered pockets of wilderness, and there are a handful in captivity. The Chinese have recently begun a husbandry program, but it may be too late to save this subspecies. There are now perhaps forty Chinese tigers still in existence.

CORBETT'S, OR INDO-CHINESE, TIGER (Panthera tigris corbetti)
Named after the famed hunter and author Jim Corbett, these tigers are smaller than the Bengal and their color is darker. The Corbett's tiger has short stripes, which turn into spots. It is distributed throughout most of Indo-China in the modern nations of Thailand, Vietnam, Cambodia, in parts of Burma, and down as far as Malaysia. The Corbett's tiger has the second-largest population in the wild after the Bengal, with some fourteen hundred to fifteen hundred tigers at present.

JAVAN TIGER (Panthera tigris sondaicus)
The Javan, named after its homeland, the Indonesian island of Java, is similar to the Sumatran but darker with more and closer-set black stripes. A dozen or so of the tigers were known to exist in the 1950s, but this subspecies is now considered extinct.

SIBERIAN TIGER (Panthera tigris altaica)
Sometimes known as the Manchurian tiger, this is the largest cat in the world, with recorded lengths of over thirteen feet. The Siberian has a much heavier coat than the Bengal, with two- to twenty-one-inch-long fur on the back and stomach. In summer the coat becomes shorter. The typical color is lighter than the Bengal, and the stripes are brown and narrow. The Siberian is a native of the cold, northeast regions of Asia, the probable original habitat of the tiger. It has been on the endangered list for some time, with only thirty or so animals known to exist in the wild in the 1930s. Due to conserva-tion efforts and other factors, the population in the wild is now two hundred to three hundred. In captivity, Siberians have done very well and now number well over one thousand.

SUMATRAN TIGER (Panthera tigris sumatrae)
A native of the Indonesian island of Sumatra, this tiger averages eight feet in length. It is a dark red color with cream-colored areas and has long black stripes often in double layers. The Sumatrans suffered from massive habitat destruction and uncontrolled hunting. Their total number has dropped by half in the last decade, years after the tiger's endangered status was known to the world. There are now five hundred to six hundred Sumatran tigers left in the wild, and their future is uncertain.

The Nature of the Beast

The tiger is a hugely built creature, with extremely powerful muscles. The head is rounded and catlike, with a heavy, vaulted skull. The tiger's ears are small and rounded. The large and powerful teeth are set in a jaw of enormous strength, giving the animal a bite of extraordinary force. The tiger's whiskers vary in density from males to females, longer and heavier in males, slighter in females. Vision in tigers is acute, but only under particular conditions. The design of the eyes gives the tiger a wide-angle view, important in the forest with its crowded vegetation and narrow visibility, but the tiger has difficulty in discerning objects that are motionless. It can detect the slightest movement of another animal's ears, but if the other creature remains still, particularly at night, the tiger may easily pass it by. Luckily for the tiger at any rate, most vulnerable prey is not smart or brave enough to keep from moving in the midst of the great predator.

Like all members of the cat family, the tiger has excellent night vision, of great importance to a nocturnal hunter. The tiger has a round pupil rather than the vertical slit of the domestic cat, but otherwise the eyes work much the same way in the dark. Like the camera lens that is opened or closed depending on the amount of light available, the tiger has its own photoelectric cells, called a tapetum, *altering the size of the retina as the light changes. The notion that a tiger's eyes turn fiery red in the dark is a myth based on the reflection of light*

BRINGING THE DEAD TIGRESS OUT OF THE POND.

lingers, other tigers will sniff the area and hurry away, realizing that they are in another tiger's territory. The pungent scent markings serve to prevent violent confrontations and to map out the area in which an individual tiger can hunt without competition from its own species.

The tiger's most developed sense is undoubtedly its hearing, which is acute. Using this sense, the tiger is able to pick up the slightest sound in the forest and is able to distinguish between a leaf rustling in the breeze and one brushed by another animal. It can even distinguish the noises made by different species, ignoring the animals it has no interest in or coming to immediate attention if he hears the sound of its preferred prey. In the days when tigers were hunted by man, tigers became familiar with the sounds of the hunters' rifles and would turn and run at the first sound of the metallic weapons.

The tiger's walk is characteristically graceful and nearly silent. It seems to glide as it moves, this smooth gait due to the almost simultaneous movement of both the legs on one side of the body and then the other. Some studies say that the tiger's steps are mathematically precise, the advancing hind foot meeting exactly the spot just covered by the fore foot. Others have measured a fractional lag by the rear foot, showing that the animal steps consistently just behind the previous print.

The pads at the bottom of the tiger's feet are surprisingly soft and sensitive and can be easily burnt or scraped open. The tiger cannot therefore move easily or at all on certain kinds of terrain. In a chase, the tiger's prey can get away by reaching ground with thorny undergrowth or bare rocks heated by a tropical midday sun. Tigers often must sit and watch while deer and other perfectly edible animals drink from a watering hole during the daytime, when the surrounding rocks would scald the tiger's tender feet. Animals with hoofs, such as the sambar (a species of deer), are well insulated to prevent such problems.

Such ironies are quite calculated by nature, intended as a means to keep an apex predator like the tiger from overkill, allowing the balance of nature to be maintained. If there were no physically imposed restrictions on the tiger, it might easily wipe out the wildlife in its area and cause its own doom. Only man has been able to ignore or outwit these natural checks and balances, with the result that numerous animal species have been hunted

caused by the tapetum. When a flashlight, photofloods, or car headlights are turned directly on a tiger in the dark of night, the reflection off the eyes does often seem to be a vivid red.

Regarding the tiger's sense of smell there is some disagreement. According to a number of trackers and some naturalists, the tiger does do considerable hunting by smell. However, the majority opinion has it that tigers do not depend on their sense of smell to find prey and that this sense is quite underdeveloped compared to its sight and particularly to its hearing. Experiments in the wild and in zoos have shown how little use is made of the scenting faculty and that tigers, unlike many other predators and large animals, cannot detect the scent of human beings. On the other hand, their sense of smell allows them to detect members of their own kind. Tigers ritualistically spray urine on certain boundary marks in their territory. Within the time the strong-smelling odor to extinction and our own habitat is increasingly dysfunctional.

Other limitations on the tiger's effectiveness as a hunter include an inability to maintain a chase. The tiger is not a runner like the cheetah, but a stalker, and will only make two or at most three springs at its prey, after which it will usually turn elsewhere. Also, the fact that the movements of a tiger on the prowl can be sensed by many of the creatures of the forest and provoke warning cries makes the tiger's hunt for prey that much more difficult.

While the tiger cannot sustain a long run, it can move at great speed. It can cover up to thirteen feet at a bound, and there are instances of tigers making jumps of twenty feet across and scaling walls more than six feet high. Going downhill after prey, one tiger on record made a spring of more than thirty feet.

The tiger's paw print—the Hindi word "pug" is commonly used—holds a great deal of information. For naturalists trying to keep track of the tiger population in a given area, pug marks will tell a cat's age, sex, weight, and sometimes even indicate the animal's mood at the time. The print is actually traced and catalogued by gamekeepers as the most practical way of counting tigers and identifying individuals among them. Each tiger's pug is unique, including the size and placement of the toes, the shape of the lobes of the pad, the top of the pad, and other individual factors. Although other aspects of the tiger would allow for individual identification, such as the facial markings and stripe patterns—both of which are unique to each individual tiger—these things do not lend themselves to practical research. The tiger is secretive and nocturnal, not an easy subject for visual or photographic identification.

Young tigers have been known to enjoy climbing trees, but this is not generally done by the considerably bulkier adult tigers. Still, they are quite capable of the occasional climb, and have been known to scale trees in order to escape an unpleasant situation, such as an attack by wild dogs, or to try and reach prey. There are cases of men climbing trees to escape an attacking tiger, only to be killed when the tiger follows them into the limbs.

Tigers are among the few cats that really enjoy the water, and many enjoy swimming or lazily floating in the water on a daily basis. This is not necessarily an instinctive habit, since tiger mothers must teach their cubs to enjoy the water. The cubs tend to make a comic spectacle as they go through the trial and error of swimming lessons. Tigers are good, strong swimmers, capable of swimming for over three miles without pausing. In parts of India and southeast Asia, tigers live a semiaquatic existence, spending most of their time in dark jungle rivers and swampy mangroves. Tigers have been known to swim from one island to another in Indonesia.

Tigers communicate with each other with a series of different calls. Roaring is a means of communicating between males and females during mating season, and much roaring is heard during an actual mating act. Tigers in general are at their noisiest when the tigress is in heat. When two tigers meet under neutral circumstances they will make a "chuffling" sound, which involves holding the mouth closed and snorting through the nostrils. In captivity, when a tiger has become devoted to a trainer or zoo worker it will also make this affectionate chuffling sound.

Another curious sound the tiger makes is called a "pook." Because the sound is similar to a cry made by the sambar, many naturalists have believed that this was an extraordinary form of mimicry by the tiger. By imitating the sambar's cry, the tiger would elicit a reply and thereby determine the deer's whereabouts. While unproven, a similar belief was held about the Siberian tiger by local hunters. The tiger was said to entrap female wapiti deer by imitating a stag's roar during mating season.

THE KINGDOM OF THE TIGER

Tigers are loners. They spend most of their lives in solitude. Tiger cubs and their mothers will live as a family unit until the cubs can safely fend for themselves. Sometimes two or more tigers from the same litter will live and hunt together for a short period after leaving the mother's den, but they will eventually go off on their own. Tigers map out the borders of their territory with sprays of urine and sometimes by marking trees with their claws. A solitary male tiger will take a very large area as his range and it will often overlap with the territory of another tiger. As long as the two tigers are not competing for the same prey, this does not necessarily lead to a confrontation. Tigers tend to concentrate their hunt for prey to a few reliable places such as water holes, making their rounds several times a day until dinner is found. Unlike the outlying areas of the tiger's territory, these key places will be defended vigorously. A tiger will, however, become less territorial when food is abundant and easily obtained.

The territory of one male tiger often crosses into the territory of several tigresses, allowing them to share common ground for mating. The tiger may mate with all of the tigresses with whom he shares territory. The tiger may also mate with just one of the tigresses again and again over a period of many mating seasons. In all cases, however, the tiger leaves after impregnating the tigress, and she cares for the litter on her own.

Among tigers, as among other species, two males will sometimes fight over a female in heat. In most cases the tiger who found the tigress first will chase the interloper off with a few angry gestures. But sometimes violence is unavoidable. A fight between tigers is a matter of ritual, with both animals exchanging a series of challenges, after each of which the other has a chance to back away. The cats stare each other in the eyes, then begin baring teeth and fanning their whiskers. As the tension mounts, the cats start to vocalize—first a very catlike hissing and then muffled growls. As the growling becomes louder and

angrier, the tigers begin slapping at each other with their front paws. When one or the other cat unsheathes his claws, things escalate, and the tigers make blood-curdling noises, standing on their hind legs and swinging wildly. The fight usually lasts only a few minutes, but some have gone on for hours. If neither tiger withdraws as the loser, the fight will end with one or the other tiger dead, usually from a broken neck. Often, the tigress will wander away during the fight and find a third male for her purposes.

Now and again, two tigers will join forces to attack another animal. There are stories of a pair of tigers attacking an elephant, or teaming up to kill a buffalo, but, if true, such incidents are not common. Although at the top of the food chain in the jungle, tigers will sometimes end up as another animal's prey. Tigers have been killed in the water by crocodiles, and packs of Indian wild dogs have been known to attack a tiger, the vicious creatures surrounding the cat on all sides and wearing it down with hundreds of bite wounds.

Death in the Wild

When dusk comes to the forest, it is time for the tiger to begin its hunt for food. The animal moves casually through its territory, checking the usual places where it can expect to find prey. On some evenings, the tiger may simply position itself in grass cover near a water hole and wait for the deer or other animals to arrive.

Once the tiger has spotted prey it begins plotting his attack strategy at once. The tiger will not approach directly, but circle around the animal. If the prey is moving, the tiger will scurry ahead and lie in wait. As it begins to close in, the tiger becomes very careful, lowering its body closer to the ground, eyes focused on the prey.

The tiger raises and lowers its head, making final calculations of the distance and angle of the prey. Then the tiger raises its body and attacks. It charges forward at full speed, front legs extended, tail tautly erect. It springs into the air. If it has calculated the proper distance from its prey, and the speed and lift of the spring, the predator hits the prey soundly with its heavy body. Often, though, despite the careful calculations before the rush, the tiger will land short and need a second leap to reach the prey. Landing from the first spring, the tiger touches the ground only long enough to arch down and propel itself into the air again for a second spring.

The tiger's thoughtful preparation for the attack is no guarantee of success. Long-term observation of cats in the wild has shown that they will make a successful kill only once for every twenty attempts. And tigers are far from persistent. If it does not catch the prey by the second attempt, it will usually turn away and continue hunting elsewhere. The tiger will have this reaction even if it has gone several days without a substantial meal.

When the tiger springs, it generally prefers to hit the prey from behind, which gives it the best angle for its typical killing method. But it will make a sideways or head-on approach as necessary. When the tiger lands on the prey, it either collapses the animal or pulls it over. Simultaneously, the tiger digs its front claws into the prey's head and shoulders and holds it down, exposing the neck to the tiger's fangs. As the prey collapses, the tiger jerks the neck violently, trying to snap the spinal cord. The tiger uses its lethal canines on the exposed neck, with a deep and well-placed bite. If the tiger has trouble inflicting a killing bite, it will press on the trachea and smother the prey. With the posture the tiger assumes at this point, it was widely believed that tigers sucked the blood from their prey, but it is not physically possible for tigers—or any cats—to drink in this way.

The precise killing method a tiger uses depends on many factors, from the timing of the tiger's attack, to the type of prey, to the experience and aptitude of the individual tiger. When attacking a large prey—such as a camel, buffalo, or elephant—the tiger may try to hamstring the creature first, disabling it and making it topple, whereupon the tiger will attack the throat. The immense size of these animals does not put the tiger off, but given a choice it will go for a smaller, young adult elephant or buffalo.

Elephant and buffalo present special problems because they are so often found in herds. The tiger has devised a form of commando tactics in such cases. It will sneak around the herd, looking to pick off a calf that has strayed. Out of fear of attack from the herd, the tiger will hit and run, killing or wounding the calf and then lying low until the herd moves on and abandons the dying or dead calf. It is a tricky business, and tigers have been killed by herds as they try to maneuver around them. When attacking an elephant, the tiger tries to rip open the animal's trunk, making it bleed to death. The hit-and-run tactic is also used on buffalo and rhinoceros calves.

Tigers have no trouble killing domestic cattle. This can become a serious problem for farmers living along the boundaries of a tiger sanctuary. Cows will wander into the tiger's territory or a hungry cat will slip into the cultivated areas. Such poaching often produces angry reprisals against the tigers, even today when the tigers are protected by law in India under all circumstances.

For such small prey as monkeys and jungle fowl, the tiger may use only its paw and its razorlike claws. It was once believed that tigers would not eat carrion or another

A DEAD TIGER.

animal's kill, but this was proven false. Still, the tiger cannot really compete for such items with the jungle's champion scavengers, the jackals and vultures.

The tiger seldom eats its prey at the scene of the kill, but drags it to a preferred spot. The great strength of the tiger's jaws is evident as it drags even huge animals for great distances. One naturalist observed a tiger drag his prey for a full mile. With a small- or medium-size kill, the tiger walks ahead, carrying it between the front legs or to the side; a heavy carcass is dragged backwards.

A discriminating diner, the tiger will take up to a half hour to prepare the meal. Like a surgeon, it removes hair and skin and tears open a section of the carcass from which to remove various body parts. It will usually begin to feed on one of the organs—heart, kidneys, liver—and move on from there, avoiding only the rumen and the viscera. The tiger's teeth do most of the work. The cat uses its claws mainly for gripping the carcass. But the tiger's abrasive tongue is quite useful in scraping every piece of meat from the bones.

Tigers are quiet eaters. During a meal the only sound is of breaking bones. The big cat will take an hour or more for dinner, eating from forty to ninety pounds of meat at one sitting. On average, a tiger needs around twenty-two pounds of meat per day, but they have been observed consuming as much as three hundred pounds in a single day. A tiger will stretch a good-size kill over several sittings. After the tiger has eaten its fill, it will cover the carcass and go off to drink or sleep until it is hungry again. Then it returns for more—chasing off whatever scavengers have appeared in the interim. Sometimes a tiger decides to prevent scavenging by sleeping atop the carcass. A large kill will last for two days, and the tiger will not begin hunting again till the fourth day. Tigers only hunt when they are hungry.

Mating

Travelers encamped in the forest during tiger mating season have come back with tales as lurid and action packed as any trashy novel. The air becomes alive with a screeching serenade, the sound of a tigress in heat and her male admirers. When the tigress's love cry draws more than one potential mate, the rivals will confront each other, sometimes in a loud and violent battle. Later, the victorious male and his new queen will mate, accom-

panied by more ear-splitting noises, a din that has been described as like "the caterwauling of a hundred midnight cats."

Although tigers pair off only for mating, during this period a form of marital fidelity exists between tiger and tigress. The male will remain monogamous while courting one female in heat, seeing no other tigresses and remaining in close proximity to the mate. Tigers live almost their entire lives alone, so social graces do not come easily to them, and the first meeting between male and female may be accompanied by a great deal of tension and much snarling and snapping. Gradually, things settle down and the couple begin to make the first series of "romantic" gestures toward each other. The tigress will nuzzle, kiss, and lick the tiger. She gives him a series of love bites and rubs herself along his flanks. The tigress becomes increasingly agitated, snorting loudly and rolling on the ground with her paws in the air. The male watches this performance with what has been described as a "surly" expression. Now the tigress gets down on her belly, presenting herself to him. The tiger moves over the tigress and, roaring mightily, mounts her. As the tiger ejaculates, he lets out a sharp cry, and sinks his fangs into the tigress' neck. The female growls back and dislodges him, quickly jumping to her feet and confronting him. The tigress will slap at the male, sometimes scratching him badly and there are more loud noises by both parties. Having chased the male back, the tired tigress stretches languidly on her side. The tiger gradually moves beside her again, attentive to her every motion. He begins sniffing her and offering tentative kisses until she springs up and moves a short distance. The tiger follows, the tigress presents herself, and the ritual begins again. It can be repeated fifty times and more in a single day, once every five to fifteen minutes or so. The actual length of each copulation is less than a minute.

This goes on for nearly a week. Tiger and tigress remain together at all times, moving restlessly through a small range, eating little. What prey they do eat may be caught by either the male or the female. At the ends of the five- or six-day marriage, the pair go their own way, the male possibly going directly to another tigress in heat.

The period of gestation is approximately 105 days. The

tigress is visibly pregnant only in the last ten days to a week before giving birth. The tigress' mate does not offer any assistance in finding food or ensuring her safety during this last, vulnerable period. The tigress finds a place with heavy cover—a cave, hollow tree, or rocks. She may have from one to a half-dozen cubs, but the average number is three, with an even ratio between males and females.

As she is about to give birth, the tigress begins licking her vulva and then pressing down at her lower half. Waiting for the delivery, the tigress either sits, with one leg raised, or stands, pressing down against the vulva until the first sign of the litter appears. As the cubs are born the tigress frees them from the umbilical cord and cleans them with her tongue. Tiger cubs are born blind. A few minutes after birth they begin crying and then move sightlessly toward the mother's nipples. A newborn tiger will weigh in the area of two to nearly three pounds and measure approximately eighteen inches from head to tip of tail. Nine months later the two-pound cub will weigh well over a hundred pounds.

With her first litter, a tigress may be awkward or uncaring with her newborns, frightened by what her body has produced. By the second and third litter, however, the same tigress will be a devoted and selfless parent. The notion that a tigress will sometimes eat her young has never been substantiated. Tiger cubs are blind or nearly sightless for their first two months. This allows the mother to keep them under control and prevents them from wandering away while she is out gathering food. When the cubs are three months old, they can begin going about with the mother, eating from her kill, and doing a lot of playful romping. There is usually a great deal of physical affection exchanged between the mother and her young.

The tigress takes seriously her responsibility for teaching the cubs everything they must know for survival. She will teach them the rudiments of stalking by games of hide-and-seek and let them practice pouncing by trying to catch her shifting tail. In the first months, the tigress continually moves her family from one lair to another, to keep the cubs safe from other predators or even from male tigers. Any intrusion on the lair will provoke a vicious response from the tigress. Many humans moving through the forest have lost their lives by unwittingly stumbling through the vicinity of a tigress's cubs.

The mother will continue to care for the cubs until they are one to two years old. At that time the young tigers go off on their own. Sometimes two siblings from a litter will live and hunt together for a while, but soon each cat takes on the solitary nature of the adult tiger.

A white tiger enjoys a summer day at the San Francisco Zoo. These days, the importation of rare animals is a complicated business. The government of the exporting country must be convinced that its own supply of the animals is not endangered.

Tigers can be as dangerous in the water as out of it. There have been many instances of tigers grabbing people out of small boats. Not completely invincible, however, tigers are sometimes caught and killed by crocodiles.

In India and parts of southeast Asia, tigers can be found in dark jungle rivers and swampy places where mangroves grow. Some tigers live a semiaquatic existence. They can swim for great distances and move from island to island.

MAN AND TIGER

Man has hunted the big cats since the time of Pharaoh Amenhotep III, over three thousand years ago. The ancient Assyrians kept lions and tigers in menageries and hunted them with bow and arrow from horse-drawn chariots. After campaigns in Asia, one of Alexander the Great's generals brought the first tiger to Europe. In 11 B.C., the Roman public got its first glimpse of a tiger at the dedication ceremonies of the Temple of Marcellus. The word tiger is derived from *tigris*, which the Romans named the striped cat after the swift and strong Tigris River of Mesopotamia.

Many tigers were brought to Rome in the time of the emperors. Emperor Heliogabalus had six tigers draw his chariot during special occasions. Tigers were the most spectacular and popular elements in the Roman arenas. The tigers and their gladiator opponents were savaged by the thousands in the Romans' beloved blood sport. The Emperor Nero became infatuated with a murderous tigress named Phoebe and had her brought to the palace and housed in a solid-gold cage. The legendary animal trainer Lybius tamed the tigress, and she later accompanied Nero everywhere and ate from his hand.

The courts of Oriental kings used tigers as executioners. A Burmese ruler kept a park stocked with hungry tigers, to which he would condemn criminals; the public was able to watch the spectacle of wrongdoers being devoured. Marco Polo wrote of the tigers used for similar purposes in the Cathay of Kublai Khan.

The Tiger Scorned

From the writings of several early naturalists and historians, the tiger got a reputation as a creature of "wanton cruelty." It was often compared unfavorably to the African lion. The lion, it was said by such observers as Sir William Jardine, had a "bold and majestic-looking" countenance, while the tiger appeared to be ever scowling and plotting assorted treacheries. The tiger's penchant for taking its prey from behind was considered an indication of a cowardly nature.

While some of the past regional potentates of India regarded

The tiger's head is huge, its neck thick and short. With a placid expression, this King of Beasts surveys its domain. Its legs are heavy and powerful, designed not for running, but for stalking.

the tiger with awe, and some made pioneering efforts to conserve their tiger population, others regarded the animal as an evil scourge. There are records of tigers being captured and tortured for the amusement of Indian royalty. Noted American hunter and author Frank Buck attended an exhibition put on by a particularly malevolent maharajah. Guests of the royal family were gathered around a walled enclosure where a declawed tiger was set upon by a pack of six wild. dogs. Like the Romans at the coliseums of old, the party cheered the cruel and gruesome spectacle, as the dogs surrounded and snapped at the tiger, its paws pained and bleeding where the claws were ripped out to give the hungry dogs an advantage.

Surrounded and in a blind fury, the tiger made a sudden and amazing leap out of the high-walled arena and into the crowd of royal spectators. Before the surprised armed guards could react, the tiger mutilated several onlookers and killed the maharajah's young son.

The pelt of the tiger has been worn as an article of clothing since the Paleolithic Era. It is only recently that the hunting of wild cats for their furs has become a large industry, with the subsequent decimation of huge populations of tigers and other animals killed for their skins.

In the days of the raj, when all of India was ruled by the British, the hunting of tigers for sport and trophy was considered the ultimate illustration of colonial majesty and domination

A family of tiger cubs. The fathers move on shortly after mating, leaving the cubs exclusively to the tigress's care. Over a period of months, the mother tiger teaches her young the various skills needed to survive in the wild.

The coloration of the tiger ranges from reddish orange to pure white. Persistent rumors of pure black tigers have never been substantiated. Because of the diverse coloration, scientists originally believed there were far more tiger subspecies.

When most people think of tigers, they tend to consider the denizens of the tropics and the Indian subcontinent. This huge, thick-furred creature hails from a very different landscape, Siberia.

of the "savage subcontinent." The tiger hunt, or *shikar*, was an occasion for spectacle, involving sometimes hundreds of native beaters, drumming the tiger into the open, and dozens of elephants, atop which sat the assorted red-faced hunters in pith helmets—who were usually well stocked with bottles of gin and picnic-basket lunches. Although the amateur hunters might often only wound a cat—and possibly turn it into a man-eater—as many as fifty tigers might be killed on a single safari.

Superstitions

In primitive tribal societies of Siberia and Manchuria, the tiger was the subject of cult worship.

Although rare, the beautiful white tiger has been found in many parts of India. Those with brown or black stripes tend to have eyes like blue ice. White tigers have been bred in captivity since the 1950s.

This Siberian appears unaffected by the snow and cold weather. Its long coat gives the cat plenty of protection against the elements. In summer the fur becomes shorter and thinner.

In some of the far northern regions of Siberia, such as Amurland, the snow lies five feet deep in winter and temperatures fall below minus-twenty degrees Fahrenheit. For this reason, the winter coat of the Siberian tiger is extremely long and thick.

The tribes believed the tiger was of supernatural origin, and it was regularly offered animal and human sacrifices. To prevent the tiger from killing humans at random, the local magicians would choose someone from the village to be sacrificed, tying the unlucky offering to a tree. To the Chinese, tigers with a particular type of face marking were believed to be the reincarnation of a human king. Throughout southeast Asia and the Malay Peninsula, there are many tribal legends regarding the transference of identities and souls between tigers and men.

In these areas, it is widely believed that a man-eating tiger captures its victim's soul, sometimes with startlingly individual results. For example, a tribe in Vietnam was plagued by a tiger that ate only women. It was believed that the marauding tiger had eaten and possessed the soul of a cuckolded husband. This rumor gave the village a long period of marital fidelity, until the tiger was killed.

Attempts are made to try and release the dead man's soul from the tiger. One method involves sprinkling roasted grains around a tiger trap, which somehow is meant to alert the soul to escape when the tiger is trapped. Animistic beliefs are still quite strong among south Asian tribal groups, such as the Minangkabau of western Sumatra. When a village has suffered an inordinate number of tiger attacks, a specialist is called in. These men are the *pawang manangkok harimau*, or, roughly, "tiger magicians." They begin their work with a thorough investigation of the village to find out whether any recent tribal activities have angered the killer cat. If the pawang determines that the tiger's attacks have been unjustified, it begins making plans to trap the animal. After requesting permission from the spirits of the forest, the tiger magician has a trap constructed in the forest. To inaugurate the tiger trap, the magician says prayers and plays tiger-capturing songs on a bamboo flute.

Silat minangkabau is an ancient Sumatran form of self-defense with similarities to kung fu, which uses movements derived from the tiger. Silat fighting masters are believed to be related to the tiger. On Sumatra and Java, there are said to be "tiger-men," black magicians capable of turning into tigers at will and spilling the blood of their enemies. Throughout the East, there are legends of *weretigers*, men transmuted into tigers, the predatory cat replacing the wolf of similar werewolf legends in Europe. In parts of India, it was once believed that kills by man-eating tigers were actually the work of evil *sadhus*, holy men corrupted by a craving

This white tiger rolling on its back looks, from a distance, playful and friendly as a backyard tabby. With careful training, many tigers have been tamed and kept as pets.

for human flesh.

In the Malay Peninsula, there have been persistent tales of villages deep in the jungle inhabited entirely by weretigers. These tiger-people lives in houses made of human skin and bone. The belief in weretigers is so strong in some regions that it has led to tragic consequences. In a village plagued by a man-eater, tiger traps were set in the surrounding jungle. One night, a man passing through the village area claimed to have been chased by a tiger and, in desperation, locked himself into a tiger cage, effectively locking the tiger out. In the morning villagers found the man trapped in the tiger cage, believed him to be a weretiger transformed, and killed him with their spears.

The image of the tiger is widely used throughout Asia as a totem against evil spirits, disease, and bad luck. Tigers are painted on the walls of Buddhist temples, on the tops of shoes, and on the swollen cheeks of Chinese children with mumps.

Among many Orientals, it is believed that various parts of the tiger have medicinal or aphrodisiacal properties. Asian pharmacists have used tiger tails in an ointment for skin diseases and mixed the brain with oil for a body rub to cure sloth. Tiger gallstones mixed with honey are sold as a cure for abscesses. Because of the tiger's prodigious sexual capacities during mating season, aspects of the animal have long been sought as an aphrodisiac. Wearing an amulet containing tiger whiskers, partic-

ularly the seventh whisker from the nose, is believed to make the wearer irresistible to women. In many corners of Asia, there is a brisk trade in "tiger penises," almost all of them counterfeited out of ox and deer parts.

Rarely has man eaten the meat of the tiger for food. Only among the Tharus of the Nepal Terai was it once considered a delicacy.

Under the Big Top

The use of captive tigers as entertainers has a long history. The Romans, of course, made sadistic use of tigers and other big cats in the arenas. In some "games," tigers were thrown together with other wild animals, while in others individuals or groups of enslaved gladiators were forced to battle the trapped predators. At other times, the Romans used tigers and lions as the public executioners of Christians and other troublemakers.

After the fall of the Roman Empire, tigers were not seen in Europe for some time, and memories of the "great striped beast" faded away. Tigers were not seen again until 1478, when one was imported to the court of the Duchess of Savoy in Turin. In the following years, other aristocrats obtained tigers for their amusement, and these menageries were sometimes exhibited to the public.

From the time of the first large-scale traveling circuses in the

This white tiger can't seem to decide whether to take a drink or a nap. The whites have fascinated people since they were first exhibited in the 1820s.

White tigers remain as rare and beautiful a sight as when they were first exhibited. A white tiger cub was once captured by the Maharajah of Rewa and kept at his summer palace. When it died, it was stuffed and given as a present to England's King George V.

The white tiger Mohini was one of the great attractions of the National Zoo in Washington, D.C., during the 1960s and early 1970s. It was said that if Mohini had been a human, she would have been the world's greatest movie star.

nineteenth century, acts involving tigers and lions have been the most popular attractions around the world. For all the hundreds of tiger trainers and "tamers" through the years, only a few men and women have mastered the art of working with jungle-raised tigers.

In the 1890s, a European trainer, Herman Weedon, trained his tigers to perform spectacular and complicated stunts and was the first trainer to bring together the tiger and lion, which are traditional enemies, in the same act. A Hungarian-born trainer, Louis Roth, came to the United States in the 1900s, working for the Al G. Barnes Circus, where his act included wrestling and riding wild tigers.

The most famous name among twentieth-century tiger trainers is undoubtedly Clyde Beatty. At the height of his career, Beatty worked alone in a cage with forty wild tigers and lions surrounding him at one time—more than were used in a full day's games at the Roman arenas.

Beatty was born in Ohio in 1905, and at age fourteen made what was then a proverbial boy's escape from small-town America—he ran away from home and joined the circus, Howe's Great London Circus, where he was assigned to sweep out the cages of the big cats. Beatty drifted to another circus, the Gollmar Bros.-Yankee Robinson, and became the cage boy for a small-time tiger trainer named Chubby Gilfoyle. His job was to dart in and out among the "man-eaters," picking up props and opening and closing the connecting cages on cue. Early on, Beatty had his shoulder bitten

In many primitive societies, there are various superstitions attached to white or albino animals. In Assam, a state of India bordering Bangladesh, villagers believe that it is unlucky, or even fatal, to kill a white tiger.

The tiger and the lion have similar skulls, although the tiger's head is heavier and more catlike. The tiger's ears are smallish and rounded. The whiskers on the tiger vary from male to female—they are much thicker on the male.

by an irritated tiger, but it was not enough to discourage him. At age seventeen, when Gilfoyle collapsed from illness in the ring at the start of his act, Beatty—like the newcomer plucked out of the chorus in an old Hollywood musical— was sent in to replace him. The teenager pulled it off, and his charismatic, improvised performance produced a standing ovation. From that time on, Beatty's became the most celebrated animal act in the world.

In the past, the European-styled tiger performances had been "still acts," with the cats formally parading and standing still in elegant tableaux. Beatty devised what would be known as the American style of tiger act, a "fighting act," full of roaring noise and kinetic, danger-ous-looking activity, with the trainer constantly moving and weaving among his fierce costars. While many circus trainers used tamed tigers bred in captivity, Beatty preferred jungle-bred tigers. He believed that tigers raised by man were not afraid of man and therefore not bluffable. He also believed the tamed, captivity-bred tigers were more obstinate and lacked personality.

Beatty was not a sentimentalist about the tigers, but he felt they should be treated with mutual respect and understanding. He never used cruelty or pain in the training of a big cat. "No jungle animal can be trained successfully by cruelty," Beatty once told an interviewer. "It'll take the maltreatment for a while, then whammy! One day the cat explodes into a raving maniac and you're done for." Beatty had a showman's skill with a cracking whip, a chair, and other objects, all used merely to catch the attention and distract the wild animals. "No one who

Tigers have a variety of different calls. Roaring is their form of communicating during mating season. They are also known to roar loudly and continuously during the actual mating.

Since the time of the Roman Empire, writings on the tiger have centered on its awesome combination of great beauty and ferocity. The animal was commonly thought to possess a "wanton cruelty."

This tiger seems to be expressing disdain for a bothersome photographer. Although there is always potential danger from any tiger, the animals have been successfully tamed and trained for work in circuses, theaters, and motion pictures.

wants to live long," said Beatty, "ever *pokes* a big cat."

Beatty seldom even raised his voice to his lions and tigers. "I don't ever shout at my cats," he said. "The animal's dignity has to be respected; you shouldn't humiliate any animal, especially not a wild one." Beatty never forgot that he was dealing with wild and ferocious animals and that they were "trained" only for as long as the cats themselves chose to cooperate. "Personally," he once told an interviewer, "I believe you can teach an animal nothing. They show you what they can do and then you develop it." Not all tigers could be expected to give the same performance. Like humans, different tigers had different personalities and abilities. Those Beatty found to have a good sense of balance he used for the tightrope walk. Those that showed a natural tendency for jumping were used in the hoop jumps or leaping hurdles. No

A noble Bengal poses at the Miami Zoo in Florida. It is difficult and costly to see tigers in their natural habitat in India. Zoos have allowed people in every part of the world to view these magnificent beasts.

After mating, the tigress may react violently to the tiger. The male reacts defensively, but both cats may be injured. This violence ends quickly, and the tigress then relaxes with her temporary mate.

two tigers were exactly alike in their disposition, and Beatty would change his style to accommodate each one. One tiger, for instance, would only follow a command if Beatty held his whip or chair in his left hand.

For many years, the exciting and "death-defying" climax to Beatty's act involved him tossing away gun, whip, and chair and staring down one of his biggest cats from a few inches away until the cat turned and ran. While audiences believed it was the ultimate illustration of Beatty's fearlessness, it was in fact something that particularly nervous animal did when *anyone* stared at him.

Beatty's circus act was famous for mixing lions and tigers together in the same cage, as Weedon before him had done. He believed that the combination of these natural enemies made things safer for him under normal circumstances, since the cats would be too wary of each other to attack the trainer. Once, Beatty *was* attacked by an angry tiger and saved by one of his lions—an event that was reported internationally. On another occasion, which Beatty would remember as the most dangerous of his career, a full-scale melee erupted between the dozens of tigers and lions in the cage. Somehow, the trainer was able to climb between the battling wild animals and crawl out with just one scratch. Guards used water hoses and blasts of ammonia to break the fight up.

As his fame grew, Beatty was sometimes hired to do his tiger act away from the circus big top. Performing at a hotel's nightclub in Detroit, Michigan, Beatty had his cats in the basement below the club. A mistake by a hotel watchman freed a Bengal tigress name Gracie. The tigress terrorized the entire hotel, bounding up and down floors and corridors. Beatty trapped the cat inside a hotel room and fought her off with a table. The cat eventually ran back down the staircase to the basement and returned to her cage.

The once-endangered Bengal tiger has become an increasing threat to people in some parts of India. Fishermen in the Sundarbans delta, prone to attack from behind, wear clay and rubber face masks on the backs of their heads to confuse the hungry cats.

This is a familiar scene to anyone who's owned a pair of housecats. Like the domestic feline, these Bengals have an obsession with cleanliness and will give each other a fairly thorough grooming.

The Sumatran tiger possesses rich ocher coloring. It is named after its native habitat, the large Indonesian island in the Malay Archipelago. Known as an "island tiger," the Sumatran is smaller than the Bengal.

Beatty was short and stocky, but with his flattened nose, flared nostrils, and cold cat's eyes, it was often remarked that he greatly resembled the handsome tigers that made him famous. From the 1930s on he was an international attraction, with his own circus, as well as leading roles in Hollywood movies and serials such as *The Big Cage* and *Darkest Africa*. "I expect one day I'll get chopped down," Beatty told a writer in the 1950s, after decades of close encounters with the big cats. "To go quick, that wouldn't be too bad. But I'd sure hate to linger on with what we call 'arena shock,' a mysterious breakdown that sometimes ends a trainer's career. You wake up one night in a cold sweat, fighting off nightmare lions and tigers. Something has snapped. The spark between you and the cats is gone and one day the collapse is complete....I hope it never happens to me." It never did. Beatty died in 1965, still the greatest of all tiger trainers.

Only a few other trainers of wild tigers achieved anything resembling Clyde Beatty's fame and success. One of these was Mabel Stock, who became a headliner with the Al G. Barnes

The tiger belongs to one of the three genera of the cat family. It is—along with such other great roarers as the lion, leopard, and jaguar—part of the Panthera genus. The other two genera, incidentally, are Felis (domestic cat, lynx, and ocelot) and Acinonyx (cheetah).

Tigers commonly make a cry called a "pook," but naturalists have been unable to say for sure what this sound signifies. Most likely, tigers use it to make their presence known to each other.

Circus, Ringling Bros., and other circuses. Her career began in 1911 and continued for forty-seven years.

She began as a trained nurse, but after witnessing a tiger act in Hollywood, she bought a Bengal from the Selig Zoo and trained with it in her backyard. Through hard work and careful observation of the tigers' behavior, Stock became the queen of her profession. Stock knew as much about the psychology of tigers as any naturalist studying the cats in the wild. In choosing a tiger for training, she would avoid cats with indications of inbreeding. Such cats, she believed, were lacking in balance and mental agility and prone to attacking without warning. Still, for all her understanding of the tigers, Stock sustained scratches and bites on every part of her body. Tigers have no control of their strength and can give as damaging a swipe with their paws in a playful mood as when angered. Stock once suffered for an entire year from a brain abscess caused by a casual slap from one of her tigers.

While performing with the John Robinson Circus in Bangor, Maine, Stock suffered her most violent encounter with the wild cats. Slipping on the muddy floor of the arena, Stock was attacked by two startled tigers. Her left leg was nearly severed, her shoulder and neck were bitten, and her face was badly slashed. After another attack in 1951, Stock lost the use of her right hand. From then on she was unable to work with a gun or chair and only wielded a whip by holding it tucked against her body. "A tiger attack comes quick and sudden—not much warning," she once told an interviewer. Like Clyde Beatty, Mabel Stock eschewed any cruelty or violence in training tigers—despite her many bloody run-ins with them. "You must bring an animal to you by your voice and manner, not drive it with clubs or whips."

The days when dozens of small and large circuses roamed the country are past. The public's reaction to the commercial use of captive wildlife has become more ambivalent, particularly when so many of the animals are on the list of endangered species. But the era in which the great cats performed under the circus big top surely marks one of the most colorful and exciting periods in the long relationship between man and tiger.

The average Indian tiger measures around ten feet from the nose to the tip of the tail and three feet from paw to shoulder. Siberian tigers are some thirty percent larger. The island tigers of Indonesia and Malaysia—some now presumed extinct—are smaller than the Indian.

One of the tigers of Bandhavgarh National Park in the Indian state of Madhya Pradesh. The park, with its large tiger population, once belonged to a maharajah. He gave it to the state in 1968, and since then extensions to the park have quadrupled its size.

IN TIGER LAND

The zoo in Delhi, located in one of the older sections of the Indian capital, has none of the state-of-the-art, imitation ecosystem exhibits of modern, wealthier city zoos, but nevertheless it draws a good crowd. Standing near one of Delhi's magnificent Bengals, a male, as it paced its circumscribed world, I watched the looks of amazement on the faces of the mostly Indian children staring at the animal.

It is only in cramped and cement-laden places like these, unfortunately, that most Indians will ever see their own glorious wildlife these days. Behind the bars, the huge Bengal stopped pacing for a moment and looked at us. It made a low growling noise and then turned away. It was late afternoon, the sun's rays had turned the area a glowing amber, and shadows had begun to darken the enclosures. In the jungle, the tiger would be rising at this time, about to begin its only work, the search for prey, the stalking of it, and the kill. It is not an easy life in the wild, even for the jungle's greatest predator, even when the wilderness areas of India were untamed and well stocked with prey. But it did not appear that the life of ease and the steady food plan in the zoo were adequate compensation for the zoo's lack of freedom. The caged Bengal looked saddened and defeated.

Much of the best work in saving and strengthening species on the endangered list is done at the world's zoos. And zoo people believe that by allowing the public to see the magnificent creatures of the wild, they raise the public's consciousness about animals, as well as inspire monetary contributions that will aid their research programs. This is all to the good, but too often zoos are a sad reminder of a shrinking animal kingdom. They have now become museums, exhibiting rare works of art, rather than transplanted glimpses of a thriving, faraway wilderness.

In the old days, when there were few restrictions on the capture and transport of wild animals, a zookeeper could write out a want list and have the desired animals caught and shipped back to order. The main problem then would be to keep the animals alive in an artificial environment. Now the situation has nearly reversed itself. Many species are now extremely rare or extinct in

A Bengal makes an impressive leap from rock to rock in the Ranthambhore National Park, India. Despite its size and weight, there is no doubt that the tiger can move with great speed and grace.

the wild. Many researchers never work with the animals in their natural habitat. Life in captivity for an animal such as the tiger is a necessary but nevertheless sad state of affairs.

At that moment in the Delhi Zoo, gazing at a morose Indian tiger, it seemed to me that for a few of nature's creatures, the benevolent imprisonment of a zoo is almost too high a price to pay for survival.

I took a last look around the tiger compound and tried to picture myself in the wild and face to face with a creature of that size and strength, with no bars or barriers between us. My next stop in India was a national game park in Rajasthan, and seeing tigers in the wild was exactly what I expected to be doing in a few days. Watching the zoo cat's huge, heavy paws, seeing its fangs and the size of its bite when it yawned, I wondered if I was doing the right thing after all.

The Journey

It was still dark when I left my hotel for the Delhi railway station. The streets leading up to the station were already clogged with people. Laborers and street people milled about in their white T-shirts and their white crosshatched *lungis*; they lined up at the numerous steaming tea wagons for buns and glasses of tea premixed with milk in tall metal containers. They looked as sleepy as I felt. The floors of the train station had been cleared. By night hundreds of homeless Indians crowd into these stations. The ground becomes a carpet of human beings. In the hour before dawn they begin to slip back outdoors.

Observing the daily life of any of India's cities makes it immediately apparent that the country's resources are strained to the breaking point by the vast population. This state of affairs also illustrates the great amount of strength and sacrifice involved for the Indian government to save the country's wilderness areas and its unique wildlife. The arguments continue, and the solutions

Tigers tend to be solitary creatures, meeting with their own kind only for mating purposes. They will, however, "socialize" at a site with a plentiful food supply and will share a kill without complaint.

This Bengal in Ranthambhore National Park, India, has just noticed the pursuing photographer and does not look pleased. Tourists in the game parks have been attacked and killed while stalking the great predator.

The tiger's teeth and jaw muscles give it both biting and crushing power of a deadly force. When attacking its prey, the tiger will generally first try to bite the other animal's neck or throat.

A tiger strides along a road in Ranthambhore National Park, Rajasthan, India. It's evident from the tracks in the road that it gets plenty of automobile traffic, most of the vehicles carrying tourists through the park.

The combination of the tiger's markings and the high grass and leaves of its habitat allow the tiger to be camouflaged from its prey.

have yet to be found that will satisfy everyone. But at the time India's serious conservation efforts began twenty years ago, the country was looking at the imminent extinction of the Bengal tiger, the nation's national animal and for some the spirit of the country itself.

I boarded the train that would take me to Sawai Madhopur, pulled out some books and magazines, and settled in. It was not supposed to be a very long journey, but on an Indian rail trip you never know. On the Indian railroad, scheduled times of departure and arrival are something along the lines of a fairy tale, a lovely

When a tiger is crouched and hidden in the forest, you may not see the creature until you are within a few feet of it. Combined with the fact that the tiger prefers to strike from behind, a walk in a tiger preserve is a very dangerous prospect.

story but not something to believe in. A train I took once from Madras to Delhi arrived three days late, and no one on the train crew could even figure out why.

The train began to move, and I caught glimpses of ancient battlements and brand-new highrises. Soon, though, the cityscapes faded away, and the train entered the Indian countryside. We were headed for Rajasthan, in northwestern India, and the first leg of the transit to Ranthambhore National Park. Rajasthan is the Land of the Kings, and one of the most colorful and distinctive areas in all of India. The state's capital city, Jaipur, is like a vision

When the tiger locates its prey, it may begin a stealthy approach, lowering the body as the sighting becomes more distinct. The tiger's head moves back and forth as it makes a final calculation and focus before charging.

A heavy splash follows as this huge Bengal explodes through the water in pursuit of a sambar. If a tiger does not catch its prey on the second or third pounce, it may give up the chase.

Two sibling Bengals react as one, tongues hanging out simultaneously as they gaze at their evening meal. Pairs of tiger brothers will sometimes live and hunt together for a time after leaving the care of their mother.

Remarkable for a cat, the tiger has a good degree of speed and accuracy when charging through the water. Deer and other animals cannot move as smoothly in the water as on land and are easily caught by the big cat.

The tiger dives into a lake and goes bounding after dinner in the form of a sambar. Tigers know that the waterways within their range are likely places to find food.

out of the *Arabian Nights*, with its buildings of pink sandstone, bejeweled camels, and its palaces, several of them now in use as luxury hotels. The north is desert country, but most of the state is very dry. For years Ranthambhore had been suffering from a severe drought, which had again put the wildlife in the park in jeopardy. Then the rain came, a monsoon that swelled the forest with water and filled the reservoirs. The wilderness reserve began to thrive.

At Sawai Madhopur

I arrived at Sawai Madhopur only ninety minutes off schedule—not bad, considering. I stopped by the Project Tiger office in the bustling town, where they helped me find accommodation for the night. Some of the Indian tiger reserves are far from being set up to accommodate visitors except in the most spartan circumstances, but Ranthambhore has several places to stay and improvements have been made as the flow of tourists has increased.

The most impressive lodging is undoubtedly Jogi Mahal, a rest house just inside the park grounds. It is a handsome, russet-colored building, once the hunting lodge of the maharajahs. Set at the foot of a high cliff and surrounded by forest, it is fronted by a lotus-studded pond, which draws deer and tigers. The Jogi Mahal has only a few rooms, however, and it is usually booked up well in advance. I stayed instead at the recently renovated Sawai Modhpur Lodge,

Lakes such as this one in northern India provide the tiger with a wide variety of prey. Besides the sambar, there are monkeys, peafowls, chital, and wild boar.

55

A Bengal tiger chases a sambar calf across an Indian lake. On the average, a tiger chases its prey for about two minutes, and one out of every five chases ends with a successful kill.

midway between the town and the park. This too was formerly a maharajah's hunting lodge, and the structure and grounds are beautiful. The vintage furnishings and old black-and-white photos on display evoke the romantic past, the glory days of turban-wearing royalty and adventurers wearing pith helmets. A swimming pool in the gardens helps one to forget the more recent past of a dusty train ride.

Tourists are allowed to go through the park only at certain times, from 6:30 to 9:30 in the morning, and from 3:30 to 6:30 in the afternoon. These are the times when the animals are most visible, particularly the first hour in the morning shift and the last in the evening. Only a certain number of vehicles are allowed into the park for each viewing period. I had arrived in time for the afternoon game-viewing excursions and was able to secure a seat in a Jeep

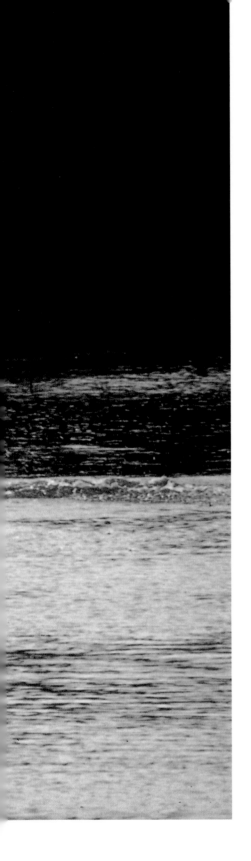

This tiger, ever the careful hunter, is in methodical pursuit of a sambar, a type of deer. When it believes the timing is right, the tiger will make a splashing charge at the helpless animal.

It has been said that tigers are "addicted" to water. They will enter almost any body of water and often for no reason other than the pleasure of it.

A Bengal tiger will roar when it has made a kill, and tigresses let out a somewhat softer roar when they are in heat. In general, tigers are at their noisiest during their mating season.

This Bengal has chosen to relax in a particularly muddy water hole in Ranthambhore Park in northern India. Of course, such a bath is for cooling-off purposes, not for bathing. The heat in this area of India can be ferocious all year long.

driven by one of the park rangers.

The Jeeps are open on top and at the sides, something that caused a moment of concern for one of the passengers. Wasn't there a chance that a tiger or some other predator could attack us and we would be totally unprotected in the open vehicle?

"Tigers do not attack Jeep," said Ravi, our driver. "It has never happen. Tigers in Ranthambhore very peaceful with people. No problems."

But later that evening I learned that Ranthambhore's reputation for no man-eaters was only relatively spotless. There had been a few unfortunate incidents over the years, and at least one killing marred the park's record. This had occurred during the time of the Ganesh Fair, when thousands of people make a pilgrimage to the Ranthambhore Fort. A young tiger that had been making its way toward a water hole in the late evening became agitated by all of the activity. When the tiger found his route blocked, it attacked, killing a seven-year-old boy and eating part of the body.

Knowing as much—or as little—as I did about tigers and leopards at the time, I too would have felt a little less vulnerable with a roof over my head as we went through the sanctuary. Ranthambhore did have a reputation for a large and benign tiger population. They were said to have lost all interest or concern in the presence of humans in their territory. But the man-eater story was proof that any time you mixed people with free-ranging tigers, the

The tiger often finds its prey near streams and watering holes. Its paws lack the insulation of other animals, however, and in areas where the rocky ground becomes broiling hot the tiger will let its prey drink unmolested.

The tiger's stripes allow it to blend in with reeds and elephant grass. It can remain inconspicuous until some prey is within reach of attack. In the evening hours, the tiger's prime hunting time, the black stripes make it difficult to see the animal even while it is moving.

possibility for a violent encounter would always exist.

"What are our chances of seeing a tiger?" I asked the ranger, as we entered the park.

"Very good to excellent," he said. "Ranthambhore has some forty-two tigers and they are quite active."

Ranthambhore covers 150 square miles of varied wilderness terrain. Can the park officials really keep track of every tiger?

"Yes, yes, each individual tiger," said the ranger. "Records are kept. Pug marks are traced, identifying size and features of individual tiger."

We moved along one of the gravel roads that weave through the park. The Jeep slowed down as we moved toward a group of monkeys at play in the road. These animals got little response from our group. In India, monkeys were nearly as common a sight as pigeons in New York. You find them at train platforms and outside temples, chattering panhandlers looking for handouts. Then a heavy-antlered deer appeared, moving slowly in our direction from the woods to the left. This was cause for more interest. The animal was beautiful to look at, and deer are the favorite prey of the tiger in Ranthambhore. Another six or eight moved toward the lake ahead.

A seven-month-old Bengal cub closely follows its mother. Tiger mothers are solely responsible for feeding their offspring at first. Not until the cubs are a year old are they fully capable of hunting on their own.

A Bengal runs across its domain in India's Ranthambhore Park. This national park encompasses 158 square miles. Tourists are taken through the park in Jeeps and other rough-terrain vehicles.

The park is a magnificent and magical area, partly bushland and rocks and partly dense forest. The huge banyan trees are some of the largest in India, and there are numerous waterways, rivers, lakes, and man-made lily ponds. What makes the landscape of Ranthambhore truly a unique and dazzling location among India's wildlife parks are the scattered, enchanted remains of the Mogul and Hindu past—the palaces, tombs, pavilions, and the huge Ranthambhore Fortress. Some of these ruins are nearly a thousand years old.

At one time, Ranthambhore was the center of a Hindu Kingdom and the scene of spectacular pageantry and bloody battles. When the armies of Allaudin Khilji invaded in 1301, the women of the kingdom barricaded themselves inside the fort and committed mass *sati*, or ritual suicide. The Mogul emperor laid siege to the fort in 1569, and for forty days and nights the

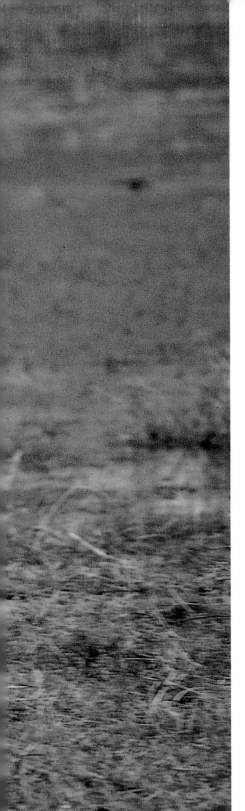

opposing armies fought and died. Now, the palaces and battlements they fought for are overrun with weeds and shrubs, and they have become the prowling ground of tigers and leopards. Ranthambhore is a rare reversal of the usual evolution: Here, civilization has been squeezed out to make room for the wildlife. In fact, some sixteen villages were depopulated for the good of the tigers, and the human residents relocated outside the park.

We stopped at another lake and saw a marsh crocodile, perhaps ten feet long, basking at the water's edge. We moved on and found a huge herd of a hundred or more chital wallowing in the water. It appeared to be a tempting sight for any hungry tiger, but still there was no sign of the great predator. A Mogul tomb loomed up, empty and haunted looking, overgrown with pipal trees. We moved toward the area known as Bakaula. After a while, the ranger stopped the Jeep. He listened to the cry of some animals not far away. We moved on, slowly.

The driver's cry, when it came, startled us all: "Tiger!" Heads turned in every direction. The ranger pointed ahead to an area between two trees. It took a moment of concentrated staring to see what he had spotted at a glance. Ears showed above the grass and then a few inches of orange and black. The figure emerged more clearly into view. It was awesome—powerful looking and beautiful. It looked in our direction, stared directly at us for several long seconds, studying us, and I felt myself stop breathing. Then the tiger lowered its head and moved on. A second later it had disappeared.

"Are we going to follow it?" I asked the ranger.

"Not now," he said. "It is a tigress, just coming from her cubs, I think. The tigress put the tiger cubs in hiding place while she goes to hunt for food. If we go near cubs now it can be dangerous."

The ranger turned the Jeep around, and we started on our way back to Jogi Mahal and the entrance to the park. Night was coming, and it was time for Ranthambhore's human visitors

In Ranthambhore National Park in northern India, a Bengal rests beside a freshly killed sambar. A tiger will stay close to the kill, and sometimes sleep directly on top of it, to protect the food from scavengers, crows, and vultures.

to clear out.

That night, I learned more about the tigers of Ranthambhore. After nearly two decades of protection, the tigers' behavior has changed noticeably, in some ways calling into question long-held scientific assumptions about the species. Are tigers truly nocturnal, or has this been an adaptation to circumstances? Tigers in Ranthambhore have for some years become diurnal, hunting in broad daylight. Their secretive, solitary lives may also be something other than instinctive. Close, long-term observation of Ranthambhore's tigers has also shown tigresses to be less secretive with their cubs than was known before. And, even more surprising, there is evidence of tigers living as complete families—the normally absent male tiger living contentedly with tigress and cubs. In the decades ahead, as tigers continue to live under the protective umbrella of the reserves, we may well gain a much deeper and more comprehensive understanding of tigers.

The next morning, shivering in the cold dawn, I was back in Ranthambhore, the first rays of sunlight casting a dreamlike glow

A mother tiger looks on as her two cubs play. Tigresses are very protective of their young, evident in this one's baleful gaze at the photographer as she ascertains whether or not the intruder means harm.

A stunning portrait of the predator in midsnarl. When attacking their prey, most tigers will rush it from up to eighty feet, grabbing it at the back of the neck with its fangs. If the prey is not subdued easily, the tiger may shift its fangs to the creature's throat.

A typical tourist's-eye-view of a Bengal tiger inside Ranthambhore National Park, India. This park is one of the world's greatest for tiger spotting. The tigers are relatively plentiful and active during the day.

across the pale Mogul ruins. After only a short time in the park, near a gorge of lush greenery, we stopped. A full-grown tiger was crouching just off the road ahead. Coming toward it, heedless, was a large sambar. Everyone in the Jeep was silent, cameras poised, realizing what was about to happen.

And it did. The sambar moved closer, and the tiger exploded into action. Two lengthy bounds and then it sprang, covering the back of the deer and bringing it to the ground with a heavy thud. It took only a few seconds for the tiger to position itself, plunging its fangs into the sambar's throat and then biting and strangling it. The deer looked dead, but the tiger clung to the throat for more than a minute. It then bit a deep hold in the carcass and began dragging the kill with great effort, a few feet at a time, moving it into the undergrowth and out of sight.

The people in the Jeep sat for a time in silent astonishment. The cycle of life and death in Ranthambhore carried on.

A female tiger in Ranthambhore National Park, in the Indian state of Rajasthan. As part of Project Tiger, an effort to save these magnificent creatures, many villages and thousands of people had to be resettled outside the park's boundaries.

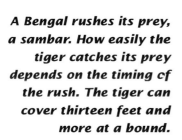

A Bengal rushes its prey, a sambar. How easily the tiger catches its prey depends on the timing of the rush. The tiger can cover thirteen feet and more at a bound.

JIM CORBETT AND THE MAN-EATERS

Jim Corbett was the father of modern wildlife conservation in India, and a man whose name will be forever linked to the vivid and dangerous world of the Indian tiger. Corbett's life was a series of ironies. He was an Englishman, loyal to the British Crown, but born and raised in rural India. He visited England only once in his life, and only for a matter of days. He was an ardent and prescient conservationist who became famous as a tracker and hunter of big game. He was a defender of the rights of the tiger and the first to warn that the great predators were becoming endangered. Yet he achieved legendary status by killing a series of voracious man-eaters. He was a modest man, with no ambitions beyond the simple life of his village in the Himalayan foothills, and yet, late in life, he authored a series of books that would become worldwide best-sellers and merit critical comparisons to Ernest Hemingway and Rudyard Kipling.

Early Years

Edward James Corbett was born in 1875 at the Himalayan hill "station" of Naini Tal. His father, Christopher, was the local postmaster. The Corbett family had a long history in India, and several of Jim's older relatives had been killed during the Sepoy Rebellion of 1857, when native Indian troops had turned against their British rulers. In the racist and rigidly class-conscious society of the British raj, Corbett's people were what was known as "domiciled English," that is, English colonialists who were born and bred on the subcontinent and thus something less than desirable for important jobs or for membership in the more exclusive country clubs and social circuits.

Jim Corbett took little or no notice of these establishment snubs, and far from seeking the blessings of the local aristos, he regarded many with a dignified disdain, particularly when they

A Bengal gallops after its prey, a calf that has strayed from its buffalo herd. The rushing attack is the last stage in the tiger's sometimes elaborate pattern of stalking its prey.

This Bengal tiger is waiting for the precise moment to spring on its prey. Hidden by trees and bush, the tiger is often able to get very close before attacking, increasing its chances of success.

committed inept or wanton slaughter of the local wildlife. Corbett's interest was in the creatures of the jungle and the Indian villagers, whom he described in his writing as "simple, honest, brave, loyal, and hard-working."

Corbett's father died when Jim was four years old, and his mother was left to bring up a full dozen children. The family had a summer house at Naini Tal and another ten miles downhill at Kaladhungi, but they were otherwise poor, living on the father's small pension. A loner by inclination, Jim stayed away from the crowded households as often as possible and spent much of his time soaking up the lore of the jungle. The wilderness began practically at the Kaladhungi doorstep, and Corbett would go out hunting to feed the family. Because of their financial straits, Jim was not allowed to waste bullets on the sort of aimless sport hunting

Sighting his prey, this tiger exhibits the typical stealth and concentration of the species. Moving slowly so as not to alert the prey, a tiger can advance for a half hour and more before pouncing.

indulged in by so many in the area. Like the tigers he came to observe and admire, Corbett only hunted to eat.

Hunting the Man-Eaters

His young adult years were uneventful. At age seventeen, he took a job with the railroad, typical employment for the "domiciled" Englishman. He worked as a middle-level inspector, overseeing rail trans-shipments across the Ganges near Varanasi. He stayed with the railroad for twenty years, but whenever possible would return to the wild Kumaon Hills of his boyhood. His knowledge of the jungle and tracking skills were renowned in the area, and beginning in 1906, local British administrators as well as the Indian villagers themselves would request Corbett's help in catching man-eaters. A typical village petition read in part, "We the public venture to suggest that you very kindly take trouble to come to this place and shoot this tiger and save the public from this calamity. For this act of kindness the public will be highly obliged and will pray for your long life and prosperity."

Corbett did not take such requests lightly. He would only go after a tiger when it had proven itself to be a habitual man-killer. He would not hunt a tiger if there had been only one or two attacks on humans, since he believed that most tigers— despite the popular belief of his day—would not attack man under normal circumstances, and most cases of a tiger taking a human life involved an accident or a tigress protecting her cubs. Corbett was not willing to hunt and punish a tiger for these regrettable but natural occurrences. Even the habitual man-eater, Corbett understood, behaved not out of some predisposition toward evil or hatred of humans—things commonly believed at the time, even by educated British officials—but out of desperation. "A man-eating tiger," he wrote, "is a tiger that has been compelled, through stress of circumstances beyond its control, to adopt a diet that is alien to it. The stress of circumstances is, in nine cases out of ten, wounds and in the tenth, old age."

Corbett's first man-eater, and his most famous, was the Champawat tigress. This one cat had killed more than two hundred

The tiger's reputation as a bloodthirsty killer is partly responsible for its decline. People have destroyed the fabled beast without compunction. In the past, tigers were also hunted and slaughtered for their pelts.

A handsome Bengal pauses at a clearing at Corbett National Park in India. In this pose, it is easy to see the close relationship between the tiger and the domestic cat, all part of the Felidae family.

However similar they may look at a casual glance, in fact no two tigers are marked exactly alike. Their facial markings and stripe patterns individualize one tiger from another, although the most practical method for researchers to identify them is by their paw prints.

75

Tigers are loners. Although some researchers have believed that tigers sometimes hunt as couples or in families, the preponderance of evidence shows that the great majority of tigers live a solitary existence.

The combination of high grass and the tiger's coloration and markings can make the animal almost invisible as it moves through the forest or stalks its prey.

A Bengal photographed on the run in Corbett National Park, in the Indian state of Uttar Pradesh. The park is named after Jim Corbett, the legendary British tiger hunter turned conservationist. Originally called Hailey National Park, it was established in 1936 and renamed after Corbett's death.

The tiger's expressions are fascinating in their variety. Here, one exhibits high excitement with bulging eyes. The eyes afford the tiger a wide-angle view, but in the forest—where visibility is often limited—the tiger depends much more on its acute hearing.

people in Nepal before drifting across the border to India. There, it killed another 234 victims at the time Corbett took up the hunt. When he arrived at the village in Kumaon where the tigress had claimed her last victim, he found a virtual ghost town: Everyone in the village was locked inside their homes, and families were huddled together. No one had gone outdoors for nearly a week, as the tigress roamed over the village road, petrifying the residents with its roaring. It is no exaggeration to say that when Corbett finally shot the tigress of Champawat, he became an instant folk hero to the people of the entire region.

In the next thirty-five years, Jim Corbett would agree to hunt another eleven man-eaters, cats of nightmarish ferocity, such as the Talla Des man-eater, the Muktesar man-eater, and the man-eating Leopard of Rudraprayag. His reputation for bravery grew, and to the local population and visiting sportsmen alike he was considerably larger than life. Corbett, as always, remained modest about his skills. "After a lifelong acquaintance with wild life I am no less afraid of a tiger's teeth and claws today than I was the day that a tiger shooed...me out of the jungle in which he wanted to sleep," Corbett wrote, referring to a childhood adventure. "But to counter that fear and hold it in check I now have experience that I lacked in those early years....Experience engenders confidence, and without these two very important assets the hunting of a man-eating tiger on foot, and alone, would be a very unpleasant way of committing suicide."

A mother and her babies rest together. Newborn cubs weigh a few pounds and gain weight rapidly. The long-held belief that a tigress will abandon her cubs if they are handled by humans has been disproved.

The tiger in the wild is, to be sure, a dangerous creature. But tigers, unlike most lions, can be scared off from attacking a person, particularly if it is unfamiliar with humans and doesn't know how easy they are to catch and kill.

As can be seen in this photo, the tiger's markings act as excellent camouflage in landscapes such as this one, the tall grass of northern India. The tigers sits patiently, waiting for an appropriate prey.

As Corbett's fame grew he was continually asked to organize large-scale *shikars*. He would be invited to share space on the elephant of the visiting potentate, governor-general, or viceroy in hunts that would involve many hundreds of men and animals—elephants, *mahouts*, beaters, and guests. Such spectacles had nothing in common with Corbett's actual style of tracking, painstaking and isolated, and always with a purpose besides mere sport.

Hunter Turned Conservationist

Corbett lived an ascetic life. He never married, and after leaving his job with the railroad and returning to Kumaon, he lived most of the rest of his life at the family house at Kaladhungi he shared with his sister Maggie. When hunting a man-eater, he would walk through the jungle for twenty-five miles with hardly a stop and go two or three days without eating. After 1930, influenced by Fred Champion's book, *With Camera in Tiger Land*, Corbett exchanged his hunting rifle for a still camera and then a movie camera. Only then, he felt, did he begin to observe and truly understand the behavior of the tiger. At the time, very little was known about the secretive and solitary tiger, and most of Corbett's written observations about the nature of the big cats were innovative and ultimately proven to be highly accurate.

Beginning in the 1930s, Jim Corbett took on the role of public spokesman for the cause of

Without a moment's delay, a Bengal tiger begins to devour a sambar immediately after making the kill. It can eat over forty pounds at one meal.

wildlife conservation. He had become keenly aware of the dwindling numbers of tigers and other species since the time of his youth. His efforts established India's first national wildlife reserve, located in the Kumaon Hills. The ninety-nine square miles of park land opened in 1936 as Hailey National Park, but in 1957, two years after Jim Corbett's death, the park was renamed Corbett National Park in his honor.

During World War II, after a period spent training British officers for jungle survival, the sixty-four-year-old Corbett became disabled by malaria and pneumonia. Confined to his bed, he began writing to pass the time. His first book, *The Man-Eaters of Kumaon*, detailing some of his legendary tiger hunts, was published in 1944 to great acclaim and was eventually translated into twenty-seven languages. For all their life-and-death situations, Corbett's stories had none of the machismo and blood lust typical of other big-game hunting memoirs. He wrote with a calm, reflective tone—revealing that when the time came for him to make his killing shot, sometimes after a hunt of many months, he felt less satisfaction than regret. In his prose, he was always ready to digress from the main hunt topic with a comic anecdote, character sketch, or mysterious piece of jungle lore. Corbett seemed to have a photographic memory and recalled the tiniest details from incidents of twenty and thirty years before.

He wrote five more books, including *The Man-Eating Leopard of Rudraprayag* (1948), *My India* (1952), and *The Temple Tiger* (1954), all of which were successful. Although many of the

These two Bengals do not, apparently, see eye to eye. The tiger is naturally solitary and will chase away intruders to its territory. Tigers distinguish and identify one another through sound and smell as well as sight.

Two tigers engage in a snarling confrontation. Tigers must sometimes defend themselves against their own kind. Fights are usually based on competition for territory or one tiger trying to appropriate another's kill.

Like most great predators, the tiger has both tremendous strength and perceptivity of its environment. The tiger is one of the most secretive of beasts, allowing it to use the advantage of surprise in catching its prey.

The tiger's strength and killing power can hardly be exaggerated. Along with its powerful teeth and jaw muscles for biting and tearing apart its prey, the tiger's claws are razor sharp and its fore legs have enormous muscular strength for gripping.

A male Bengal tiger emits a warning growl. Naturalists have been able to catalog an array of tiger expressions and sounds. They can differentiate between the warning growl prior to attack and one made before withdrawal.

Tiger "pug" marks are evident in the mud near the Ramganga River, India. Pug is the Hindi word for an animal's footprint. From a pug print, naturalists are able to judge many things about the tiger, including sex, age, and weight.

Conservation efforts in India have proven very beneficial for the tiger. However, local villagers near such preserves as Dudhwa National Park have not pleased. In that area alone, nearly five hundred villagers have been killed since the park was created.

stories were about the hunting of man-eaters, Corbett was as often as not the defender of the great predators. "Tigers," he wrote, "except when wounded or when man-eaters, are on the whole very good-tempered. Were this not so it would not be possible for thousands of people to work as they do in tiger-infested jungles, nor would it have been possible for people like me to have wandered for years through the jungles on foot without coming to any harm."

To this day, a local legend persists that the spirit of "Corbett Sahib" protects the people of Kumaon.

Unlike the lion or the jaguar, the tiger has a fairly high tolerance for a variety of habitats. Its size, coat, and color are adapted to the ecosystem in which it lives.

TIGER RESERVES OF INDIA

The boundaries of India contain the greatest number of tigers in the world. After the centuries of sport hunting and habitat destruction, there are now strict laws prohibiting any activities that would endanger the country's tiger population. The concept of wildlife conservation and game reserves is not a new one in India. Its roots are over two hundred years old, dating back to the third century B.C., when Emperor Ashoka decreed the creation of many wildlife sanctuaries. India now has over three hundred national parks and sanctuaries, with over a dozen important tiger reserves.

The tiger reserves of India are spread out in various regions of the country, in every sort of terrain. Many have nearby accommodations and transportation facilities to bring tourists through the reserves, but others many are difficult for visitors to reach and have little or no tourism facilities. To visit some of the areas, special permission must be obtained from the local wardens. In all of the tiger reserves, there are various regulations, strictly enforced, in order to maintain a thriving tiger populace and to eliminate the chance of violent encounters between man and animal. Unfortunately, and despite plenty of warnings, some visitors confuse wildlife parks with amusement parks. A number of tourists, as well as local villagers, are mauled or killed by tigers in the parks each year. The following is a list of the leading tiger reserves, with more planned to open in the near future. With the exception of Royal Chitwan National Park, in Nepal, all are in India:

BANDIPUR TIGER RESERVE
In the forests of Karnataka, formerly Mysore, this park was established in the 1930s and greatly expanded in the last decades. Tigers share the area with a large elephant population.

BANDHAVGARH NATIONAL PARK
This was once the private property of the Maharajah of Rewa. The

This white tiger enjoys a bath in this cool pond several times a day. Tigers are good, strong swimmers, and one of the few big cats to actually enjoy the water.

A tiger takes advantage of the smooth road cleared for the tourist vehicles in Ranthambhore National Park, India. Because of the economic importance of tourism, the Indian government has done much in recent years to improve visitors' amenities.

area was noted for a high incidence of white tigers, some of which have made their way to zoos in America and Europe. The park land was extended in recent years, and it has one of the most well-equipped tourism centers, the Bandhavgarh Jungle Camp, at the park entrance. Located in the central Indian state of Madhya Pradesh, the park is closed during the summer monsoon season.

BUXA TIGER RESERVE
In West Bengal, this reserve has been under the administration of Project Tiger since 1982. The tigers share the area with large herds of migrating elephants.

Tigers mark their territory by spraying a strong-smelling secretion from under the tail. The remaining odor from the spray is meant to indicate the tiger considers the area its exclusive hunting ground.

A tigress gives her cub an uncomfortable-looking ride. Tiger mothers are devoted to their young, keeping an almost constant watch over them until they are around one year old.

A mother tiger comforts her three-week-old cub. Baby tigers are born blind with eyes shut, and the mother must hide them from predators while she goes out hunting. After three to five days, the eyes of the cubs usually open.

A cub contemplates his photographer. Young tigers are extremely frisky, leaping about and exploring everything in their range. They are particularly fond of tree climbing at that age.

A tigress keeps an eye on her cub in Bandhavgarh National Park, India. To ensure the continuation of the species, the park is closed to tourists during the tigers' breeding season, the months of July to October.

CORBETT NATIONAL PARK

Named after naturalist-author Jim Corbett (there is a noble-looking bronze of the great man at the park), it was originally established as Hailey National Park in 1936 and was India's first important national park. It was in this area, at the foothills of the Himalayas, that Corbett tracked and shot many a notorious man-eater. Of the park's 201 square miles, more than half is considered the core, to be left totally undisturbed. The park has approximately one hundred tigers, and they are occasionally seen strolling down the road used by visitors' vehicles. The hills of Corbett have a substantial leopard population, which generally stays as far away from the tigers as possible. The park has a plentiful supply of some of the tigers' favorite form of prey, with four varieties of deer available. There are good facilities here for visitors, with elephants available as transport through the park. This provides a safe and natural way of observing wildlife, and the view from on top of the elephant is excellent.

DUDHWA NATIONAL PARK

Although the area was fought over by a number of conflicting interests, Dudhwa has become an important sanctuary for tigers. Tigers were reintroduced to the area thanks in great part to the work of a legendary figure in the area named Billy Arjan Singh. The sanctuary was originally established to protect the swamp deer, but Indian rhinos as well as tigers have benefited. Comfortable and exotic accommodations are found at the farm on the southern boundary known as Tiger Haven.

A tiger cub enjoys a water hole in Bandhavgarh Park, India. Although tigers are among the few cats to really enjoy the water, it is not necessarily instinctive. A tiger mother usually teaches her cubs to enjoy it, through the trial and error of swimming lessons.

Tiger cubs are pampered and protected by their mother until they are about six months old. Only then do they begin exploring on their own, but still not more than one hundred feet from the watchful maternal eye.

INDRAVATI NATIONAL PARK & TIGER RESERVE

Project Tiger became involved in this park in 1983. It is another reserve located in the large state of Madhya Pradesh. The park has a huge core area of nearly five hundred square miles. The landscape is made up of huge expanses of teak and bamboo forest. Besides tigers, Indravati is an important homeland for the wild buffalo.

KANHA NATIONAL PARK

Kanha is a rich green area of forest and valley, parts of which have been a sanctuary since the 1930s. Project Tiger has done much to make this a thriving area for tigers and other major wildlife species. A successful relocation program was undertaken, moving a large number of villages out of the park. At the turn of the century, tiger hunting in the Banjar and Halon forests was done here by the British Viceroy and others from the colonial hierarchy. Khana has been called the greatest of all the Indian parks.

MANAS TIGER RESERVE

A stunningly beautiful reserve, hosting twenty species of birds and a variety of animals on the Endangered Species List, Manas is bisected by the Manas River and stretches along the border between India and Bhutan. Project Tiger keeps elephants for visitors to ride through the park. There are many tigers, but the reserve is difficult to reach.

MELGHAT TIGER RESERVE

In an area of dry teak forest, Melghat was one of the first tiger reserves set up by Project Tiger in 1973. It has one of the densest forests of any of the reserves, so the viewing of tigers here is not ideal.

NAGARJUNASAGAR SRISAILAM SANCTUARY & TIGER RESERVE

With 1,374 square miles, this is the largest of the tiger reserves. It has a wide range of habitats, from tropical thorn and bamboo forest to dry scrub, in an area full of deep gorges.

NAMDAPHA NATIONAL PARK

Located in the state of Arunachal Pradesh, close to the border with China, this is the northeasternmost domain of the Bengal tiger. This is the only park containing India's three major predators: the leopard, the clouded leopard, and the tiger. The alpinelike forests at the highest areas of the park are some fifteen thousand feet above sea level. Being in such a remote and inaccessible part of the country, Namdapha is little visited and therefore completely unspoiled.

PALAMAU TIGER RESERVE AND SANCTUARY

Here was the site of the world's first tiger census, in 1932. It was also one of the first reserves brought under the auspices of Project Tiger. The habitat is made up largely of sal forest and bamboo.

A pair of white tigers, Hema and Hari, warily circle each other. The courtship rites of tigers are often bumpy. The male and female will repeatedly approach each other, exchanging blows until they have gained each other's confidence.

A mighty yawn for a mighty
animal. Most tigers in the wild
are nocturnal hunters, looking
for prey between dusk and dawn
and sleeping in the daytime.

A study in contrasts, a Bengal with the typical brown and striped coat passes behind the much rarer white tiger with black stripes. Despite the distinct color differences, the two tigers could come from a single litter.

PERIYAR TIGER RESERVE
This is the southernmost sanctuary for the Indian tiger. The park was first established in 1934. The elephant population is large, while the small number of resident tigers are very elusive.

RANTHAMBHORE NATIONAL PARK
This park, in the arid state of Rajasthan, is perhaps the best location of all for seeing tigers. This is because the tigers have lost their shyness or fear of humans and—uniquely—can be seen being active and even hunting during the day. The park has a colorful setting, being the one-time center of a fourteenth-century Hindu kingdom, with the remains of a beautiful fort. Tigers can sometimes be seen climbing among the historic ruins. There are more than forty tigers in Ranthambhore.

ROYAL CHITWAN NATIONAL PARK
This was formerly hunting ground for Nepal's ruling family and is now an important sanctuary for tigers, rhinos, and other species. It has some of the most elaborate facilities for visitors, including the legendary Tiger Tops Lodge, with its spectacular wildlife views.

SARISKA TIGER RESERVE
Sariska was once the property of the Maharajah of Alwar. Ironically, it was the maharajah's love of elaborate tiger hunts that kept the area undeveloped and a haven for the big cats. There are now more than forty tigers in the reserve. Tigers here are strictly nocturnal, unlike those in Ranthambhore.

As far back as the 1950s, naturalists declared that the tiger population was in danger of extinction from hunting and destruction of its habitat. Yet it was another two decades before serious work was done to save the tiger.

With its serene pose for the camera, it is hard to believe this Bengal lives in the wild. But it is not atypical of the relatively passive behavior of tigers in Ranthambhore National Park. They have become used to the presence of people in their realm.

One of the rare tigers of Bannerghatta National Park, India, enjoys a self-grooming session. The park, established in 1974, is less than twenty miles from the city of Bangalore, and is relatively small at forty square miles.

SIMLIPAL TIGER RESERVE AND SANCTUARY
An area of sal forest, full of rivers and waterfalls, this was once the hunting reserve for the royal family of Mayurbhanj. It became one of the earliest sanctuaries to be taken up by Project Tiger.

SUNDARBANS NATIONAL PARK AND TIGER RESERVE
This is a large reserve made up largely of swampy wetlands. Here the tigers are breeding more successfully than anywhere else, and there are more than four hundred tigers in residence at present. The tigers are considered unusually ferocious here, and there have been many inexplicable attacks on humans. Unusual measures have been taken to try and curtail the number of tiger attacks on the local fishermen and others.

A tree in Bandhavgarh National Park, India, shows the marks of a tiger's territorial tree scratching. The tiger will stand on its hind legs as it pulls its claws through the wood. The practice is not consistent among tigers—some do it regularly, others not at all.

This young tiger lets out a happy, healthy roar. He is one of the big cats of Melghat game reserve in India's Maharashtra state, allowed to thrive thanks to the aid of Project Tiger.

This huge Bengal appears ready to do some tree climbing. Actually, tigers do not particularly enjoy climbing trees. As adults they are too bulky to make a habit of climbing, but they have been known to scale a tree in order to catch someone perched in the branches.

A Bengal tiger in heated pursuit of a sambar, photographed in Ranthambhore National Park. In the wild, every tiger must be a skilled hunter, finding, stalking, and killing the prey.

This tiger has just spotted the photographer and is reacting to the perceived threat. Tourists in the Indian game parks who have gone on foot in pursuit of pictures have ended up mauled or killed by threatened tigers.

Perched on a rocky vantage point, a tiger keeps close watch on its surroundings at Kanha National Park in the state of Madhya Pradesh. Green and hilly Kanha is known to tiger lovers as the single best place in the world to observe these beautiful creatures.

An Indian tiger stops for a drink at a water hole at Ranthambhore Park. The big pond at this northern Indian game park draws large herds of deer, the favorite prey of the local tiger population.

A royal Bengal fords a stream in northern India. The tiger will take to the water to cool off on a sweltering afternoon or simply to romp about. They can swim over distances of three miles without pausing.

A tiger quenches its thirst at a northern Indian riverbank. Not unlike their smaller cousins, the domestic cat, tigers are very clean, even fastidious. Tigers never urinate or defecate in water.

A Bengal tiger stretches out beside a riverbank. In much of the tiger's Indian habitat, the midday heat can be scorching, and it enjoys cooling off at the water's edge. It has a particular fondness for the cooling spray of a waterfall.

This Siberian tiger prepares to spring on its prey. The tiger is a fierce and determined hunter and will attack creatures its own size, such as the Siberian brown bear and the Himalayan black bear.

It was long believed that tigers' eyes turned a burning red at night, but this is inaccurate. It is actually the reflection of light, such as a car's headlights, that gives the appearance of bright red eyes.

Tigers, like domestic cats, are territorial. Each male's territory overlaps with that of many females, which encourages mating. The male tiger may mate with all of the tigresses within its territorial range.

Although the Indian tiger's habitat can be one of the more sun-baked regions of the world, the tiger does not thrive in the heat. When forced to exert itself in the midday sun, the tiger can be seen panting, tongue lolling from its mouth.

An Indian tiger partially consumes a buffalo in Bandhavgarh National Park. After a kill, the tiger will drag it to some safer spot for eating. In the case of a buffalo, this can mean dragging a carcass of over four hundred pounds.

The tiger walks with characteristic grace. The smoothness of this Siberian tiger's gait comes from the almost simultaneous movement of both legs on each side of its body, as well as the way its hind foot meets almost exactly the spot covered by its fore foot.

This royal Bengal looks like it has just swallowed some very unpleasant-tasting medicine. Photographers' telephoto lenses now allow us to get an intimate view of the tiger's every gesture without disturbing it.

SAVING THE TIGER

The status of the tiger has been greatly improved in recent decades. Twenty years ago, tigers in the wild faced complete worldwide extinction. The dawning realization that these unique and beautiful animals might cease to exist galvanized an international effort to save them, with governmental, organizational, and individual contributions of labor, money, and ideas.

Much has been done since the beginning of that initial period of enlightenment. But much more remains to be done, and projections by population-biology theorists suggest that the chances of the tiger living another century remain slim. The work that has been done in the past twenty years has only been a stopgap, extending the species' life but not guaranteeing their future. Several tiger subspecies have become extinct. It has been only a few years since the Javan and Balinese tigers faded into legend. The Indonesian government had taken measures to protect the remaining animals, but it was too little, too late. The Javan tiger, which had traditionally symbolized nature's power, now symbolizes nature's fragility. Efforts are now under way in the Soviet Union and in China to save their dwindling tiger populations. It seems highly unlikely that the tiny number of Chinese tigers left will ensure that subspecies' survival. The future of the Siberian is equally dispiriting.

The passing of laws to protect the tigers and the establishment of regulated tiger reserves is not enough to guarantee protection. Many of the reserves in India may prove too small or isolated for their tiger populations to reproduce successfully. When a reserve is surrounded by cultivated farm lands and human populations, the tigers are isolated, in essence trapped. This can lead first to deadly fights over territory. Secondly, it leads to the elimination of genetic diversity. Under ideal circumstances, young tigers would leave the area where they were born and eventually mate with tigers from other areas, expanding the genetic mix. When hemmed in, these tigers begin mating with family members, parents with offspring, brother with sister. Such continued inbreeding eventually leads to fewer offspring, a susceptibility to diseases, and other problems, eventually leading to self-destruc-

There are now only a few hundred Siberians like this one in the wild, and most are under the protection of the appropriate governments. The Soviet Union has done the most to protect the Siberians in their natural habitat.

White Bengal tigers, like this one, can be part of otherwise normal Bengal litters. The white's unusual coloration is a result of a mutant gene. They occur as partial albinos, with white fur and gray-brown stripes, or, more rarely, with an all-white coat.

A sturdy white tiger strikes a noble pose. The tiger is the largest feline on earth and has been reported to eat as much as three hundred pounds of meat per tiger in a single day.

This Bengal tiger is one of the stars of the Cincinnati Zoo. In addition to its success with breeding captive tigers, it is also the site of innovative and important work in the field of embryo transfer in exotic cats.

This Bengal, cooling off in an Indian pond, looks comfortable enough. Much has been done to protect the reduced population of tigers in the world, but in the long run the survival of the species remains in jeopardy.

The tiger's natural surroundings are re-created as closely as possible at the Hyderabad Zoo in India. This Bengal tigress romps with her offspring.

Although tigers are native to many regions of India, they are as exotic and fascinating to that country's people as to the rest of the world. The great majority of Indians have seen tigers only in captivity, such as at the Hyderabad Zoo.

This Siberian tiger kitten is just three weeks old. It was born in a zoo. If efforts to save the Siberian in its natural range fail, the confines of a zoo will be the last refuge for the subspecies.

tion.

Poaching continues to be a problem in national parks and reserves. While most nations now have strict laws against the import or export of tiger skins, many of these are still confiscated at airports each year. Farmers risk large fines to rid themselves of a marauding tiger or simply to sell the skin to a dealer for a high price. The tigers are shot or, more often these days, poisoned with a deadly odorless chemical called *endrin*. Also, the legal and illegal destruction of forest resources puts a continuing strain on the tiger's habitat. In India, more than three million acres of forest are lost each year.

Even with the best of intentions toward the tigers, India's government must deal with the demands of a growing human population that now numbers over seven hundred million. The

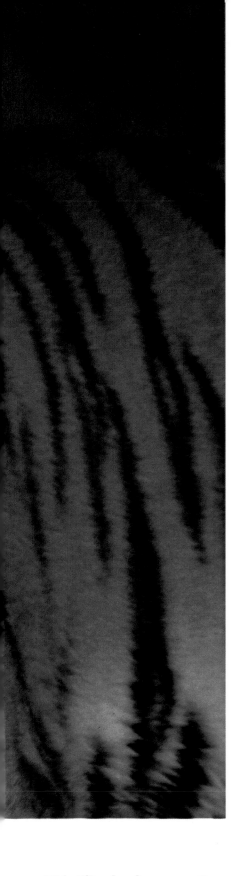

This Siberian is among the residents of the Minnesota Zoo. With its harsh winters and heavy snowfall, Minnesota has a climate roughly comparable with that of Siberia and northern China, to which this species is indigenous. It is sometimes critically important for the zoo to re-create a captive animal's natural habitat.

tiger problem can only really be solved by finding answers to the human problem. As Nepal's Hemanta Mishra of the King Mahendra Trust for Nature Conservation put it, "Without meeting the basic needs of food, fuel, fodder, and shelter for impoverished farmers outside the boundaries of tiger sanctuaries, there may be no tigers or wilderness areas left to protect." Nepal and its tiger population has an even more intensified problem than India. A mere fourteen percent of Nepal's land area is arable. Due to the Nepali topography, it is plagued by deforestation. In the midst of this land crisis, it becomes all the more difficult to maintain sizable chunks of potential farm land for the preservation of a small number of tigers.

Recent Developments

Tigers vary in size according to their subspecies. The largest of all, as pictured here, is the Siberian. Both male and female Siberian tigers can grow to over twelve feet in length and weigh over six hundred pounds.

Happily, the tiger's future does not look entirely bleak. There are many signs of hope in the world of tiger conservation, and scientific developments may soon be able to increase immeasurably the tiger's chance of survival.

Researchers and captive-breeding specialists have been experimenting for years with techniques for the artificial insemination of tigers. On April 27, 1990, at the Henry Doorly Zoo in Omaha, Nebraska, the world's first tigers conceived by in-vitro fertilization were born. The sperm of a white male tiger was mixed with the eggs of a Bengal tigress and implanted in a

nine-year-old Siberian surrogate mother named Nicole. Delivered by Caesarean section, the litter consisted of a white male cub and normal-striped male and female twins. The white male died shortly after birth, and the male twin expired some months later, but the third cub is healthy and growing at this writing. With this breakthrough, scientists can now look forward more optimistically to a time when the same artificial-insemination process can be done in the wild, allowing genetic exchange and replenishment among the tiger populations in the reserves, particularly those in tightly circumscribed surroundings.

With the dwindling wild populations of all subspecies except for the Bengal, the future of the tiger in the wild has been left almost entirely to the government of India. Whatever scientists come up with in other parts of the world, it will still depend on the cooperation and interest of India and the Indian people.

Project Tiger

I asked R.L. Singh, the director of Project Tiger in New Delhi, about the degree of his country's commitment to the tiger—now and for the future.

"We started Project Tiger in 1973, when there were 1,827 tigers left. Now we have 4,335 tigers in India. Some 28,017 square kilometers of our forest has been reserved, established as

*A **Siberian tiger** crosses a snowy expanse in the far northeastern region of the Soviet Union. Its thick coat of fur is an adaptation to the fiercely cold weather of its homeland.*

A rare and beautiful white tiger displays gemlike blue eyes. While some of these tigers' coats are actually pure white, most are striped brown or black on white, cream, or eggshell white backgrounds.

tiger reserves. About 3,600 people are permanently employed to look after these tiger reserves. Our investment in the maintenance and preservation of the reserves is around 200 million rupees per year—entirely met by taxpayers' money, so there is no foreign assistance labeled for this project."

The biggest problem in maintaining the reserves has been "the people in these areas," according to Singh. "Tribals have been put to disadvantage with the establishment of these tiger reserves. And people in these areas have not been getting a due share in developmentary schemes when near the reserves, because we were not allowing construction of roads or buildings or any irrigation projects that would benefit these villages. One of our major schemes is to rehabilitate 120 tribal villages which are still located in the tiger reserves. We will translocate them by giving land equal to the land they are occupying. We have already shifted forty-two villages."

Another program intended to alleviate tension among the people living on the reserve

White tigers like this one have done well in captivity. In fact, for some the tender care at a zoo has extended their life expectancy. A number of captive tigers have lived to be twenty, five years above average.

Mating between tigers usually occurs during the daytime. There are no tiger "couples," and the tigress in heat mates with any available tiger. While copulating, the tigress knows it is in a highly vulnerable pose, neck exposed to the tiger's practiced death bite.

borders is called Eco Development. It is a compromise program. "Outside tiger reserves," Singh explains, "we will start commercial forestry operation, and only local people will be allowed to take the forest produce from that area. They will then have a stake in the preservation of the tiger. We will lose some forest from that area, but the government is of a mind that there should be a happy human buffer around the tiger reserves."

Regarding the future of tourism at the reserves, Singh says that it "will be very strictly regulated. It is not going to be encouraged in the core tiger reserves. The idea is that these should work as gene pools. [In such areas] no unregulated tourism is allowed, no grazing cattle allowed, no tourist complexes are to be constructed. People are allowed only from 7 A.M. to 9 A.M. and 4 P.M. to 6 P.M. No one is allowed to move on foot, [only by] strictly regulated vehicular

A white tiger strikes a peaceful pose. Tigers brought up in zoos are, not surprisingly, much more docile than those raised in the wild. But as any zookeeper can attest, even the seemingly tamest tiger can be dangerously unpredictable.

White tigers have been bred in captivity for some time. The process of specifically breeding for white tigers can lead to a number of genetic peculiarities, however, including crossed eyes.

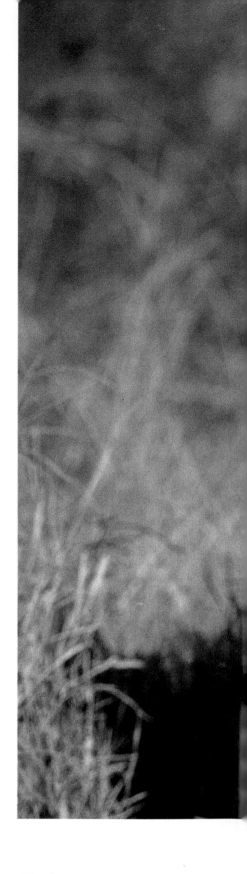

These two Siberians are contented residents of the Cincinnati Zoo in Ohio. Although Siberians originated in a unusually harsh and isolated area of northeastern Asia, they have bred quite well in captivity.

movement on specified park roads. Free-ranging tigers need very special monitoring, care, and management. We have established veterinary-care centers in each tiger reserve, as well as research centers."

The government of India has funded Project Tiger for at least the next five years. Two more tiger reserves are planned for the near future, one in Uttar Pradesh and another in Gujarati.

"It is an important mission," says Project Tiger's director. "The tiger is India's national animal."

And the tiger, Singh says firmly, will survive.

The tiger does not grow a mane like the lion, but an older tiger will have a ruff of long, thick hair on its cheeks. In fact, the lion and tiger have much in common and are closely related—the closest kin in the cat family.

131

In the late afternoon, this tiger is found resting at the water's edge. Soon it will be up again and roaming the forest in search of prey, the never-ending challenge of life in the wild.

A distinguishing characteristic of the Siberian tiger is the male's much broader muzzle, or front part, of the skull. It is overall much bigger than the typical Bengal.

The tiger in the middle plays a somewhat disgruntled pillow for three other Bengals. In the wild, one seldom sees groups of more than two tigers socializing. Those that do are usually families.

The Sumatran tiger is becoming an increasingly rare sight. This "island tiger," native to a large island in Indonesia, has seen its population dwindle in the last dozen years. There are only about five hundred Sumatrans left in their homeland.

This Bengal demonstrates one way of entering the water. Tigers love all water, but they seem to prefer fresh water to salt. Scientists believe that too much salt water may irritate the tiger's liver.

Compared to the Bengal tiger, the Siberian has longer, softer, and paler fur. The cat pictured is also a resident of the Minnesota Zoo.

This tiger's paw may look harmless enough in repose, but don't try offering it a handshake. Even without its claws extended, a swipe from this Siberian's powerful limb is deadly.

The tiger takes a cooling drink. Access to water is of great concern to the tiger, not just for drinking but for cooling off in the sweltering tropical climate. When forced to move in the heat, the tiger tends to pant heavily and dangle its tongue outside its mouth.

Siberians were in grave danger of extinction not long ago. Even now their future is in question. Naturalists must continue to work to ensure that the Siberians' gene pool is varied enough to produce healthy tigers.

One of the Siberian tigers at the Minnesota Zoo pauses for water. The pool it is drinking from is actually one of the zoo's ingenious "invisible" moats, which keep different species separate.

It was not until the 1960s that white tiger specimens were seen in the zoos of America and Europe. A zoo in Washington, D.C., and another in Bristol, England, featured the rare cats, which became the sensation of their day.

There are approximately two hundred to three hundred Siberians left in the wild, yet a minimum of two hundred and fifty are necessary to continue a sound genetic blend.

A white tiger stands in full view, allowing a rare glimpse at its magnificent fur coat. Humans have long coveted this beautiful covering, and until the 1970s the tiger-fur trade was a significant factor in decimating the tiger population to the point of possible extinction.